Child of the Fifties

Child of the Fifties

A Memoir

Kenneth C. Dewar

Rock's Mills Press
Rock's Mills, Ontario • Oakville, Ontario
2024

Published by
Rock's Mills Press
www.rocksmillspress.com

Copyright © 2024 by Kenneth C. Dewar.
All rights reserved. No part of this publication may be reproduced, distributed, or transmitted in any form or by any means, including photocopying, recording, or other electronic or mechanical methods, without the prior written permission of the publisher, except in the case of brief quotations embodied in critical reviews and certain other noncommercial uses permitted by copyright law. For permission requests, contact the publisher at customer.service@rocksmillspress.com.

For information about trade, library, and bulk orders, please contact the publisher at customer.service@rocksmillspress.com or through our website.

To Marged, Megan, and Helen

Contents

CHAPTER ONE. Introduction | 1

CHAPTER TWO. Growing Up Modern | 7

CHAPTER THREE. Camping and Character | 31

CHAPTER FOUR. Paperback Reader | 55

CHAPTER FIVE. The Sixties | 77

CHAPTER SIX. Innocent Abroad | 103

CHAPTER SEVEN. Decisions, Decisions | 131

CHAPTER EIGHT. Last Word | 161

ACKNOWLEDGEMENTS | 167

NOTES | 169

INDEX | 178

Chapter One
Introduction

> Yes, it was [the sixties], but as I said, it depended on where—and who—you were. If you'll excuse a brief history lesson: most people didn't experience 'the Sixties' until the Seventies. Which meant, logically, that most people in the Sixties were still experiencing the Fifties—or, in my case, bits of both decades side by side.
> —Julian Barnes, *The Sense of an Ending*[1]

There was no single moment when I decided to write a memoir. The idea came on me gradually. Looking back, I can see how one thing led to another, though the temptation to see an underlying purpose, retrospectively, in what were actually discrete moments and events is one to be avoided. If there was any connected development, it was in a growing consciousness of my personal relationship to public events. This may seem an odd thing for a professional historian to say, but for a long time I thought my interest in history was academic, not just because I was a professor, but because history for me was a subject of study, "out there" in some fundamental way. This runs counter to the view that historians are always personally implicated in the things they write and teach, and that the arguments they make and the conclusions they arrive at—and even the topics they choose to study—are all inescapably the result of their commitments in the present. Carl Becker, an eminent historian of the European Enlightenment and the intellectual origins of the United States—which is to say, a historian of the transatlantic Enlightenment—delivered a famous presidential address to the American Historical Association in 1931, "Everyman His Own Historian." Everyone, he says, writes from his own present, and his own present shapes the resulting history. Years later, J. H. Hexter, a historian equally prone to chart his own path, countered Becker by arguing that a historian's sense of the present was just as likely to be shaped by his knowledge of the past as the other way around. I found Hexter very persuasive on first encountering him, I think because of my detachment from my subject.[2] I've become less certain of this as the years have gone by.

I first began to think seriously about my relationship to the 1950s quite by accident in 2003, when an old friend, Dale Miquelon, invited me to participate in a conference in Saskatoon dedicated to the life and work of Hilda Neatby. Dale and I had first met in the early 1960s when we were both undergraduates at the University of Alberta (he was two years ahead of me), and then later at the University of Toronto as graduate students. He became a historian of New France and spent his career at the University of Saskatchewan. Neatby was also a historian, of Quebec after the Conquest, though she had made a public name for herself as a member of the Royal Commission on National Development in the Arts, Letters and Sciences—known more commonly as the Massey Commission, after its chair, Vincent Massey—and as the author of a scathing critique of progressive education, *So Little for the Mind* (1953). She had been a distinguished member of the Saskatchewan history department, chairing it for a number of years just before Dale's arrival in 1970. I had written an essay on *So Little for the Mind* that had appeared in *Queen's Quarterly*, and Dale and his colleague Michael Hayden, who had edited and introduced a collection of Neatby's essays and reviews, were organizing the conference, which they called "Hildafest."[3] It was to take place in March 2004.

I had a schizophrenic relation to Neatby, it must be said. I was interested by—and admired—the moral force that animated her critique of progressive education. She wrote with great intensity, arguing that the underlying purpose of education was to instill in children an awareness of western society as the product of Judaic morality, Christian love, Greek philosophy, Roman law, and modern humanism.[4] She did not believe education In a diverse society should be religiously based, but neither should it call into question the virtues of honesty, duty, generosity, and humility. She quoted the American muckraker

Lincoln Steffens, who testified that the turning point of his life had been the moment when he realized "that *the world was more interesting than I was*."[5] This was a view that served to keep pride and self-regard in check, rather than giving them free rein as progressivism seemed to do, and it undercut the authority of "experts" (always referred to by Neatby in disdainful quotation marks).

At the same time, I had some sympathy with the aims and methods of progressive education, having adopted some of them in my own teaching, and having joined in efforts to reform the graduate program in the history department at the University of Toronto in the late 1960s along progressive lines. I thought small discussion groups a critical part of teaching, designed to encourage students to become "active learners," and I tried to combine them with a conventional lecture format. I also became involved in a variety of radical causes that Neatby would have found deeply offensive. I did not share her belief in the primacy of western civilization but rather welcomed the acceptance of a multiplicity of cultures and the multiplicity of narratives that displaced the coherence implicit in the idea of a single civilization's narrative.

Another feature of Neatby's critique that had attracted my interest was its implicit nationalism, or perhaps more accurately, its provincialism. Progressivism, after all, was American in origin and its leading proponent was the leading American philosopher of the time, John Dewey. Neatby believed that the American model of democratic pragmatism, personified by Dewey, was one to be avoided by Canadians, a belief shared by Massey, who would have included education among the matters taken up by the Royal Commission had it not been an area of provincial jurisdiction. He later encouraged Neatby and gave her financial support. The conservative nationalist George Grant, who rose to prominence in the fifties and sixties as a critic of American influence on Canadian politics and foreign policy, had a similar outlook. His views were grounded in religious belief, as were Neatby's, and both were knowledgeable about the world but neither of them was cosmopolitan in outlook. They directed their intellectual activism inward to their own society.

These different aspects of Neatby's outlook had given rise to my study of her critique of education that had prompted Dale's invitation—a reflection, in short, of my commitments in the present. I was pleased and flattered to be included among the invitees, but I said to Dale that I wasn't sure I had anything else to say about her. The conference was to be held in the Bessborough Hotel, the venerable Saskatoon railway hotel, and I joked that the last time I had been in the Bessborough was for the western regional convention of the International Brotherhood of Magicians in 1957, where I had won a small trophy for Junior Manipulation. Perhaps, I said, I should title my paper "Hilda's Fifties and Mine." This turned out to be less of a joke than I anticipated, since I ended up giving a paper entitled "Hilda's 1950s and My 1950s." Preparing it set me thinking about that decade, how the very serious, not to say severe, Neatby typified it in many ways, and how my own years growing up in Edmonton partook of the same intellectual and cultural milieu.

It was one of the most satisfying academic projects I ever embarked on, partly because of the direction in which it led me, and partly because of the conference itself. Over the course of a day, a dozen speakers were featured, some of whom I knew quite well, including Neatby's nephew Blair, whom I had first met in the early 1980s when I had spent a year as the Marston LaFrance Post-Doctoral Fellow in the History Department at Carleton University; Don Wright, whom I had met as a member of the council of the Canadian Historical Association and who was working on his biography of Neatby's contemporary, Donald Creighton; Allison Prentice, whom I had known since the 1970s and who was a historian of education and women's academic lives; and Jim Miller, who had been a graduate student at Toronto when Dale and I had been there, and who had long been a colleague of Dale's in the Saskatchewan history department. Others I knew less well (Nicole Neatby, Paul Litt) or was meeting for the first time (Paul Axelrod, James Pitsula, Thomas Wien, and Diane Hallman), but together they made up a congenial group, and the audience, which included former students of Neatby's and other interested people, added to the mix. The day was full of interesting papers, highlighted by a lunchtime talk by Blair on the different sides of his aunt's life, and an after-dinner address by the novelist Guy Vanderhaeghe on the intersections of fiction and history.

Continuing to think about Neatby and me, I revised the paper for publication and it later appeared in the *Journal of Canadian Studies*, but only gradually did I realize the extent to which the decade had made me.[6] After I retired I decided to explore "my fifties" a little further. I wrote a couple of memoiristic essays on my undergraduate years at the University of Alberta and my later venture into the retail book trade.[7] What became apparent to me as I did so was how much my life had been shaped by an underlying moral seriousness that I had absorbed from my parents, and by a fortuitous combination of idealism, scepticism, habit and accident. At the same time, I found the larger project more difficult, partly because I was uncertain about the reliability of my memory. I was reassured on this score when I read Julian Barnes's *The Sense of an Ending*, on the recommendation of my daughter Helen. It seemed his memory was no more reliable than mine: "If I can't be sure of the actual events any more," he wrote, "I can at least be true to the impressions those facts left. That's the best I can manage."[8] This seemed a reasonable ambition. He also had a similar sense of "the sixties" as mine, as expressed in the quotation at the head of this introduction, which Helen thought sounded a bit like me.

I decided to start with memories of my youth and to work up to the sixties, when my involvement in the politics of the time evoked some of the thoughts and emotions I refer to above in describing my reactions to Hilda Neatby. I thought then that I had reached some kind of maturity, and of course I had, but however formative, it was also true that this did not represent some kind of conclusion or crystallization of character. Instead, it was a stage in my development, to be succeeded by other stages reaching down to the present. What follows, then, is less an autobiography than a memoir: in other words, a personal history of my time.

Top left: Max and Mary Dewar on the Saskatchewan River "flats" in Edmonton.
Top right: Max Dewar, early 1950s.
Bottom: Maxine, Bob, and Ken near Banff, late 1940s

Chapter Two
Growing Up Modern

Looking back on my childhood and youth in 1950s Edmonton, it seems obvious that my father's death in 1955 marked a watershed. It was momentous at the time, of course, but its significance in my life became more apparent as the years went by. I was just ten years old; he was only forty-seven. He had a heart condition, which produced a succession of heart attacks—the first in 1948, the second in 1952, a third in 1954, and the last on 1 April 1955. My mother used to say, with uncharacteristically dark humour, that the earlier ones had all occurred in even-numbered years and she had thought we were safe until 1956. Had he lived in more recent times, his condition would almost certainly have been treatable. As it was, he died in the flower of his middle age.

Over time, I also realized that there were many people beyond me and my family who were affected by it. He was the senior Edmonton partner in his architectural firm, Dewar Stevenson and Stanley, and the most important project of his career was then under way, a new Edmonton city hall. The building would not be completed for another two years and the firm dissolved around this time, Kelvin Stanley never having been a partner in the Calgary branch, Stevenson and Dewar. Before going into private practice in 1949, Dad had been Assistant City Architect, then City Architect, and his connections continued to expand. He had been president of the Alberta Association of Architects in 1945–47, and had been elected a fellow of the Royal Architectural Institute of Canada in 1954. Cecil Burgess, teacher and mentor to many of the province's architects, wrote an obituary for the RAIC *Journal*, saying among other things that Dad's death was "a calamity to the profession and to a much wider circle in Alberta."[9] There were also volunteer organizations in which he had been actively involved, including the Kiwanis Club, the Masonic Lodge, and especially the YMCA and its men's service club, the Y's Men, both of which he had served as president. His name was familiar enough in the city that the story in the *Edmonton Journal* announcing his death referred simply to "Max Dewar" in its headline, rather than more formally to his full name, Maxwell C. Dewar, or something like "well-known city architect."[10] All of this was obvious to many, as was evident in the hundreds of people who packed into First Presbyterian Church for his funeral.

One immediate result of my father's death was a family move. The previous year, we had moved from our home in the Highlands to "the south side," not far from the university, into a house designed by his firm as part of the "Trend House Program," a project of the British Columbia lumber industry under whose auspices ten houses were built across Canada by firms identified with modern design.[11] Dewar Stevenson and Stanley was selected to do the Edmonton house. The houses were supposed to be models of the future and were open to the public for a period after their construction. The thing was, ownership fell to the firm involved, which also meant that responsibility for selling it did so as well. When the Edmonton house did not immediately sell, we moved in. After Dad died, we moved back to our old house, which fortunately had only been rented in the interim, and the "Trend House" was sold, presumably for financial reasons.

The move caused a bit of an upheaval, but it was also a return to familiar territory. The house had been built in the early forties, to a design of my father's, and expanded since. It had a big backyard on the edge of Rat Creek Ravine, with a vegetable garden, crab apple trees, lawn, and a big patio. A small creek bed ran beside the house down into the ravine, which itself ran down into the North Saskatchewan River valley some distance away. There was ample room for semi-wilderness play—many games of "Cowboys and Indians." Both my brother Bob and I had cowboy hats and toy guns and holsters. A path on the other side of Rat Creek was our wintertime route to hockey practice at the Cromdale Community Rink. This move also proved to be temporary, and a few years later we moved again, presumably also for financial reasons, to a smaller house further out in the Highlands.

Another result of my Dad's death was that there were no more family holidays, which figure prominently in my early memories, particularly visits to Banff, which had been a favourite destination of my parents when they were first married. They owned a car, which apparently sat on blocks for much of the year during the Great Depression, but in the summer they made trips to Banff that were highlights of the years before my older sister, Maxine, was born in 1939. They spent their days hiking and their nights sleeping in the car, forming a bond with the mountains so close that they later asked that their ashes be scattered together in Paradise Valley, in the shadow of Mount Temple near Lake Louise. After my mother died in 1975, I hiked in with my brother Bob and his wife Vie to a point beyond Lake Annette, up from the bottom of the valley. Maxine opted out, too saddened by my mother's death to take part.

I don't know how many trips we all made together when I was a child, but they included hiking, horseback riding, swimming at the Cave and Basin (a historic complex on the edge of town where bathing involved rapid movement between activity in the cold pool and relaxation amidst the sulphurous odours of the hot springs), and trips out to the Banff Springs Hotel and the so-called "million dollar view" out over the Bow River to the peaks beyond. I have a photograph of my mother and all of us children—my father being the photographer—in the conservatory of the hotel. One year, riding horseback from the stable behind the lodge where we always stayed, I decided an exciting thing to do would be to whip my brother's horse in the hind quarters with my reins and so set us all off at a gallop. My father was not pleased, nor was our guide.

Another year—it might have been 1954—we made a big trip to "the States," south through Montana to Coeur d'Alene, Idaho and on to Yellowstone National Park and the Old Faithful geyser. Dad had just bought a new car, an Oldsmobile 98, which was a step up from his previous Olds 88, and it needed to be taken in for service after a certain number of miles, as cars did then. One morning, he set off from our motel with Maxine to the local dealer, saying that they would return with a rented car for the day. Choosing the car, Maxine persuaded him to go for a red Chevrolet Bel Air convertible, not the mechanical equal of the Olds but much snazzier and attention-getting. It was characteristic of my father that he agreed, and it was equally characteristic of my mother to be shocked when they returned, but also to come around with very little resistance. We happily set off for the day and soon ran into a rain shower, which forced us to pull over to put the top up. As we were doing so—it took us a little time—a bus full of American servicemen rolled by, windows wide open, with the guys inside waving and whooping at this picture of discomfort—and also, no doubt, at my attractive 15-year-old sister.

Such adventures would not now be repeated. Nor would the weekend trips to "the lake" that had begun not long before when we had acquired a cottage near Seba Beach on Lake Wabamun, west of Edmonton. A cottage had become available in a line of others owned by people who were friends of my parents through the Y's Men's Club and Y's Menettes (a name evocative of the time), including the Spragues, McClarys, Smiths, and Robertsons, and so offered opportunities for socializing. Life at the cottage featured swimming, motorboat rides, and water-skiing during the day and bonfires, wiener roasts, and sleepovers at neighbouring cottages at night. I later came to loathe the noise and fumes of motorboats but they were common on Lake Wabamun, as they and their various motorized descendants remain today at holiday lakes all over North America. Cottages at the lake were a part of automobile culture as well (like red convertibles) and I remember sitting in the back seat on drives to the lake, occasionally standing—standing!—to look over my father's shoulder at the road ahead. No seatbelts in those days. The fact that my mother didn't drive must have been one reason for selling the cottage, though I also doubt that she was as keen on lakeside socializing as my father.

In search of some solace, my mother felt a desire to return home to Scotland, which she had not visited since emigrating in 1924. She had come on her own (five pounds sterling in hand), to join her sister Janet in Edmonton. I knew little of Auntie Jennie, with whom my mother had some kind of falling out over the care of their own mother in her last years. I knew even less of my grandparents on either side, or of my numerous other aunts and uncles. For reasons of which I was unaware, they seemed all to have grown apart. My mother's older brother James Millar, with whom she had kept in touch, still lived in Scotland, in Kilmarnock, not far from Greenock, where they had grown up. A brother had died in infancy before she had been born and a sister in childhood just after. Another brother, Matthew, a year younger than James, had enlisted in a Renfrewshire regiment of the Argyll and Sutherland Highlanders at the beginning of the First World War and been killed in Egypt three years later at the age of twenty-three. One of the lost "generation of 1914," his memory seemed to have stayed with my mother, who had been thirteen at the time of his death. The men of the family all worked in the shipbuilding industry, my grandfather as a piece-work clerk, and in the early twenties my mother had a job as a typist at the famous firm of Harland and Wolff, whose Belfast shipyards had built the *Titanic*.

In addition to my Uncle James and his family, there were also cousins and friends my mother wanted to see. In the summer of 1956, when I was not yet twelve and so eligible for half-priced fares, she took me with her on a trip to Scotland, travelling east by train to Montreal and across the Atlantic on a Cunard liner, the R.M.S. *Ivernia*. Transatlantic air travel was still a novelty in those days. The ocean voyage took seven days, including the last leg from Liverpool north to the Firth of Clyde and the "Tail of the Bank," the anchorage at Greenock where we disembarked by tender. It was a long trip, but the length of time and the services and entertainment provided made it a world unto itself, the view from the deck alternating from fog to icebergs to the open sea as the voyage progressed. I made one or two friends during my time on board and played quite a lot of shuffleboard and ping pong, occasionally visiting the cinema.

We were met by James, who delivered us to the house of a friend of my mother's in Gourock, a town next to Greenock on Caldwell Bay. From there we spent the next three weeks or so visiting people and some of the sights of the region by bus and occasionally by boat—an evening cruise up the Gare Loch, a trip down the coast to Ayr to visit Robbie Burns's cottage, another to the resort town of Largs to meet up with James and his wife Annie. One bus trip took us to the village of Houston, where Mom's mother, Mary Barr, had been born. (Mom was born Mary Barr Millar, named after her mother.) Her family house was still standing, though a little the worse for wear, and there were cousins still in the village, one of whom recognized my mother because of her resemblance to my grandmother. A couple of days later we returned to the nearby village of Bridge of Weir ("Brig o Weir") and out to a dairy farm called Selvielands, said to hold one of the finest herds of Holstein Friesian cattle in the country. It belonged to another cousin, Robert Houston. This was all new to me, never having been on a farm in Canada, much less Scotland. It was a very tidy operation, with up-to-date milking machinery, the result of a modernization following Robert's recent marriage. Previously, when the farm had been occupied by Robert and his brother James, both bachelors, facilities had been rather more primitive, without electric power or indoor plumbing. I spent part of the afternoon watching men haying, and later, after tea, the milking of the herd.

Some of this I can relate today because I kept a rudimentary journal of the trip, written in an uneven eleven-year-old hand, and recording observations perhaps also characteristic of my age: "Never stops raining over here" (29 July). I also have some photographs, including slightly blurry images of the *Ivernia* taken as we pulled away on the tender, and better ones of Uncle James and Auntie Annie. They were both taller than my mother, plainly dressed, smiles softening faces that were already getting on in age. James was sixty-three, Annie sixty-one, my Mom fifty-two at this point. I appear in several of them, alone or with others. I think it must be a common experience of the era of mass photography for people to look upon their childhood selves and wonder just who that person was, not just in outward appearance (smiling and cheerful) but in inner disposition (apparently eager to please). One thing the journal reminds me of, reading it now, is that Mom was having problems with her health, being sick to her stomach on more than one occasion. This meant we sometimes hung out for the day at

Mrs. Bonnar's, at whose house we were staying. Once we took a trip to Glasgow to visit another cousin, Matthew Houston (brother, I think, of Bob and Jim), who was chaplain at the Royal Infirmary of Glasgow. Learning of Mom's stomach troubles, he lined up an appointment with a doctor that same day, and we later went back to the city twice more for an x-ray and a follow-up visit.

Her health may also have been a reason for our generally relaxed pace, though I don't remember that we were ever frenetic tourists on our holidays, trying to take in everything there was to see. I read a few books—Louisa May Alcott's *Little Men*, Charles Nordhoff and James Norman Hall's *Mutiny on the Bounty*, Jack Schaefer's *Shane*—and we often played cribbage or canasta in the evenings or even during the day. Some days, when we weren't going off to Houston, Bridge of Weir, or Glasgow, we stayed around Gourock, shopping or going for walks. Sometimes we went into Greenock, on one occasion visiting the cemetery where Mom's father was buried and searching out the tenement "close" on Wellington Street where the Millar family had lived. Another day we took the bus to Edinburgh, walking Princes Street and visiting the Castle, where we found Uncle Matthew's name on the Roll of Honour at the National War Memorial.

For some reason my journal ends on July 31st, the day before we were to make another trip to Glasgow to see the doctor. We also went to Kilmarnock at some point, where James and Annie lived, and at least some of their family. We spent another week in Scotland before heading south for London, where we really were tourists, taking in Westminster Abbey, St. Paul's Cathedral, the parliament buildings and Big Ben, and the Tower of London, where we ogled its famous "Beefeater" guards and the Crown Jewels. My memory of the last part of our trip is otherwise pretty vague, including our trip home on R.M.S. *Saxonia*. I do have a souvenir card with an "abstract" of the ship's log, which tells me we sailed from Liverpool on August 15th and arrived in Montreal on the twenty-first, having travelled some 2700 miles at an average speed of 19.4 knots, or 22.33 mph (36 km/h in metric terms). The trivia of record.

We arrived home to find that Maxine and Bob had survived pretty well in our absence, aided by the assistance provided by a neighbour, though I had a sense of some tension between them. Bob was thirteen at the time of my father's death and already showing signs of rebelliousness in his dress (stylish drape pants, three-quarter length jacket) and hair style (long, worn in a ducktail, with a curl of hair dropping down over his forehead). We later joked about how he used to leave for school in the morning with his hair almost soaking wet, no matter the weather; in sub-zero winter temperatures the hair would conveniently freeze into place. The classic fifties film, *Rebel Without a Cause*, starring James Dean and Natalie Wood, came out in the fall of 1955, depicting the alienation of youth in a manner that came to represent the decade. Bob was something like the James Dean figure, without the romanticization of the Big Screen, and I think my mother was totally at a loss about how to respond. When he quit school a couple of years later, took up the plumbing trade, and married young, I thought this represented, at least in part, his route to independence.

Maxine, at sixteen, had her own share of rebelliousness and she, too, quit school within a couple of years to get a job and married soon afterward. Whether intentionally or not, this was equally a declaration of independence. In both cases, I thought at the time that my father's death was a significant factor. I think Maxine's and Bob's relationship to him may have been closer because they were older. A friend of mine, one of a group of four of us who car-pooled to university in the early 1960s, became a serious psychology student, going on to do a Ph.D. The rest of us were all in humanities disciplines and were sceptical, to say the least, of psychology as a means of understanding people, individually or in groups. One morning on our way to school, Barry waxed eloquent on his latest discovery, the theory that personality is fundamentally shaped by family birth order. We were having none of it and gave him a good-natured ribbing, but I later came to think that he may have been onto something, if only because I realized that I myself might be a case in point. As the third and last born (and something of a surprise, my mother once told me), I was the "baby of the family" and had things my own way more than either my brother or my sister. While there were practical reasons for my going on the trip to Scotland, I was probably also being favoured and certainly was the centre of attention for the duration. Maxine was the archetypal first-born. This shows in a photograph I have of her when she must have been close to three and still the only child. She is standing between my mother and father, who are seated and leaning slightly forward, and she has one arm around the neck of each and a very satisfied, somewhat mischievous smirk on her face: "Look at me," she seems to be saying, "I'm in charge." She held the senior position in the family and felt some responsibility for its well-being. Bob, also typically, was caught in between.

* * * * * *

When I started to think seriously about investigating my family history, I began like thousands of others in this Age of Genealogical Research: I Googled some key words. These took me to two sites in particular, Ancestry.com and Scotland's People. The first proved especially fruitful, not because I turned up information on my own, but because I found help. Despite having worked as a professional historian for most of my life, I had rarely used the tools of demographic research and, when I had, they had taken the form of paper documents in archives and other repositories. The online sources were unfamiliar—and they cost money. Their wide use clearly belies the skinflint reputation of my ancestral people, though I tried the "14-Day Free Trial" and found that it took me only to the first layer of investigation. If I wanted to go further, to find out which of the possible names brought up by my initial inquiry was the one I was looking for, and to look at the documents that showed this—census records, birth and death certificates, passenger lists of ocean-going vessels, attestations of identity for the purpose of entering another country—I had to purchase a subscription to the site. I suppose this is not really surprising, since many people might find what they were looking for in the fourteen days and the company operating the website would make no money. I was hesitating, wondering if it would be worth my while (my genes possibly kicking in), when I had a stroke of luck.

My starting point had been a document a friend of mine had obtained for me some years before from the Commonwealth War Graves

Commission. It gave the "Casualty Details" for my Uncle Matthew: his rank (Lance Corporal) and service number, his regiment, his date of death (11 November 1917), and the location of his grave (the Gaza War Cemetery) and how to get there. Typing in his name at Ancestry.com and registering for the 14-Day Trial took me to the beginning of a family record, an account of details from the Census of 1901. There was much about this record that I did not understand; for example, that Matthew's death date appeared to be unknown, and that his father (my grandfather) was dead in 1901. If the latter were true, my mother could not have been born. As I have said, I could not get to the actual census record, but the page on the website for Hugh Paton Millar, my grandfather, had a note on it, written by another (more skilled) investigator a few years before, correcting the death date and providing an e-mail address. The address proved to be still current, and I made contact with Marna Fielding, who turned out to be a niece by marriage of one of the sons of James and Annie Millar. She had been doing genealogy for thirty-odd years, partly because her mother-in-law had taken it up as a hobby in retirement, and she had offered to help. She enjoyed it, as I soon discovered.

I believe it is through contacts such as this that many family histories (or "family trees") are constructed. The biggest surprise for me was that Marna turned up documents, not just for the Millar family but for the Dewars as well. I learned the proper birth date for my father (1907), having always known his obituary to be inaccurate in this respect. I also learned that he had emigrated in 1921, five years earlier than the estimated date I already had, and that most of his family had emigrated together: both his parents and most of his brothers and sisters. This was news to me, as well. His father had been a storekeeper, I discovered, described as "manager," and my father's "Passenger's Declaration" told me that he was in school and able to read and write, and that they were all headed for Edmonton, where there was someone identified as his uncle. Both of my parents were examples of "chain migration," following a relative or someone else they had known at home to a destination overseas. As I have already mentioned, when my mother came on her own in 1924 she was joining her sister Janet, also in Edmonton.

Child of the Fifties

I know nothing about how my parents met, except that they were both keen tennis players and both members of a Scots society in which they did highland dancing. They were also both members of church groups. Did they meet through one of these? It seems likely. I also know nothing of my father's early life; for example, whether his father's intended occupation of "Farming" given on the passenger manifest had been genuine or merely *pro forma*. I came to know something of his professional career, however, when an architectural historian wrongly attributed responsibility for the design of the Edmonton city hall in a book he wrote about Alberta architecture.[12] He said that Kelvin C. Stanley had designed the building, a claim based on signed drawings in the Canadian Architectural Archives at the University of Calgary. It was true that Stanley had seen construction through to completion after my father's death but it seemed inaccurate (and unfair) to call him "the designer." I knew otherwise on pretty direct evidence, not least of which was memories of my father coming home early in the morning after working at the office all night on the city hall plans. This was before we moved to the Trend House. I had also attended the official opening of the building with my mother in 1957, at the invitation of then-Mayor William Hawrelak, who had told me how sorry he was that Dad had not lived to see the completion of his project. I set out to correct the error, but I needed something of a more documentary nature to prove my case.

This was not difficult to find. When the design was unveiled in April 1954, the *Edmonton Journal* ran a large picture of a scale model on the front page and a long story inside under the heading "Plans For New City Hall Embody Latest Innovations." It referred more than once to "architect Max Dewar," a reference that was often repeated in "The Journal Letter Box" in the days following, often with none-too-friendly comment on the "innovations."[13] Official records showed how city council arrived at the decision to grant the city hall commission to Dewar Stevenson and Stanley, a process involving appearances by my father before council and culminating in a contract laying out the terms of the commission. It included a section stating that, since Dewar wished to give "personal attention to the actual construction" to ensure it was carried out according to plan, he was authorized to make whatever visits he thought necessary.[14] This provision was necessary because official responsibility for supervising construction was assigned to the City Architect's Department. The contract was signed by my father for the firm. A few weeks after the plans were unveiled, city council unanimously approved them, despite initial hesitations, and the *Journal* published a photograph of Mayor Hawrelak, Alderman Fred Mitchell, and my father with a scale model of the proposed building.[15] As usual, Dad is the shortest man in the picture. Finally, when the building was finished in 1957, the city published a pamphlet in celebration, in which the city hall was described as "a memorial to its architect, Maxwell Dewar."[16]

I also contacted some of the people involved. Gordon Wynn, a partner in the contemporary (and competing) firm of Rule Wynn and Rule, told a friend of whom I had made inquiries, "It's news to me if Max did not design the City Hall." Dudley Menzies, City Commissioner at the time, told me that all the correspondence between the city and the firm had been between himself and my father. Hugh Seton, an employee of my father's firm, replied warmly to my letter of inquiry, explaining that the design was the result of a team effort led by my father, who had secured the contract, taken the design forward to city council and the public, articulated its principles, and written the construction specifications. Hugh was described in some of the documents I had seen as the "Design Architect," meaning (he explained to me) that he actually developed many of the ideas and made many of the drawings, in close consultation with my father and Kelly Stanley. He then became project architect, or job captain, preparing the final drawings, which had to be initialled by a partner, as he was then an employee. This was why Kelly's initials were on the drawings in the Canadian Architectural Archives. Kelly himself responded that the reason he was identified as the architect must have been that he had taken over as spokesman for the firm after my father's death, and all contacts concerning the city hall were thereafter directed to him. He thought that people in "the media" didn't always do their homework.[17] The evidence seemed pretty clear that my father was "the architect" of the city hall by any normal use of the term. If anyone had "designed" it, by some narrower definition, it had been Hugh Seton.

As I sought to dot the i's and cross the t's (ensuring that my own professional scruples were satisfied), my interest widened to take in Dad's career and the architectural history in which it was embedded. After technical school, he studied with Cecil Burgess, who ran the architecture program at the University of Alberta, such as it was. There was no degree program at the university until the early 1930s—like other professions, such as law, architectural training had its origins outside the university—but Burgess had taught courses in architecture since 1913, and he oversaw the certification of qualified practitioners through the university and the Alberta Association of Architects. In this capacity, he taught and mentored a large number of the province's architects. My father registered in the AAA in 1930 and received his certification the following year. Others certified in the 1930s included John Rule (who formed a partnership with Gordon Wynn in 1938), John Cawston (with whom my father later partnered for a few years), John Stevenson (his Calgary partner), and Jean Wallbridge (with whom he later worked in the city architect's office and who was one of the first women to receive a Bachelor of Science in Architecture in Canada). For someone who had little sympathy with modernism himself, Burgess taught many of the major figures in the development of Alberta modernism. The degree program was terminated in 1940 because of low enrolment, probably the result, in turn, of Depression conditions.

After qualifying, my father joined the firm of MacDonald and Magoon, an established Edmonton partnership responsible for many of the buildings that shaped the city in the early twentieth century. He may have worked there at first as an articling student or junior architect. Several years later, in 1937, he was appointed Assistant City Architect and Building Inspector. I recall my mother saying that it was a relief to land a secure full-time job in the 1930s, and to leave behind the uncertainty of private practice on commission. Before long, he was working on the building for which he is now best remembered in the city of Edmonton, at least in a public way: the Rossdale Power Plant, next to the river in the "Ross Flats." This was a rebuilding and expansion of a power generation facility whose origins dated back to the turn of the century, when, in the halcyon days of municipal ownership in Canada, Edmonton Electric Light and Power became a publicly owned utility, which it still is. Presumably this is why my father, in the city architect's office, came to be put in charge, though it seems possible that his connection with the plant began in the early thirties.[18] The building that resulted became an Edmonton landmark, an imposing piece of modern classicism, innovative (at least locally) not so much in its internal steel skeleton and brick curtain walls as in the idea that industrial architecture might celebrate modern technology and combine aesthetic appeal with functional efficiency. The "Low Pressure Building," which is particularly identified with my father, comprises three large, flat-roofed blocks, sitting perpendicular to the river, their strong horizontal lines defined by white concrete cornices. Tall windows in the lower block, and small rectangular ones above them, under the white line of the higher cornice, provide full interior light and exterior definition. Seven large smoke stacks give it the appearance of a massive ocean liner.[19]

The fact that I drove past the Rossdale plant numerous times in the early 1960s, on my way to university with my carpool friends, ignorant of its connection with my father, has taken a little getting used to as I have become more aware of the extent of strong connection over the past couple of decades. At first, my main informant was one of those friends in the car, Elwood Johnson, an Edmonton lawyer who has cultivated an interest in community history, first in the Highlands, where he lived for many years with his family, then in Rossdale, where he and his wife Diane later moved. He told me of the efforts to preserve the plant and renovate it for new uses, occasionally sending along newspaper clippings, and eventually of the renaming of the Low Pressure plant as the Maxwell Dewar Building.[20] My brother Bob also sent clippings. The preservation movement, which gathered force in the 1990s and early 2000s, made me think that Edmonton, a city that I remembered as quick to tear down the old in the interests of the shiny new, had changed in this respect as in so many others in the years since I had left. I had become interested in the city hall story just at the time when it was about to be torn down to make way for a new one, which only confirmed my earlier impressions. I had not expected my father's name to be commemorated in a power plant. Proud as I was, Woody and I had a chuckle or two over the idea of the Maxwell Dewar Low Pressure Building. More recently, I smiled again at the headline of another story he sent me, quoting photographer Tim Folkmann, who was planning a light show on the side of the building: "The City Kicks the Shit Out of its Architecture Too."[21]

My father's association with industrial architecture was driven home by the example of the Churchill Wire Centre, another municipal project for which he became responsible, and which has received the attention it deserves in recent years as a result of the growing interest in the city's architectural heritage.[22] Originally built for Edmonton Telephones, another municipally owned utility, it must have been one of his first big jobs after being appointed City Architect and Building Inspector in 1944, on the retirement of the previous office holder, John Martland. Its purpose was to house switching equipment, but it was another design that integrated attractive form and mundane function, perhaps even more important since it was located in the centre of town, rather than in the industrial river valley. It was built in the style that architectural historians call "stripped classical," a variant of Art Deco in which the building's mass is diminished and made more human by slightly inset window openings—first and second floors in a single visual unit, and set in pairs—that are framed by regular, symmetrical lines of vertical columns reminiscent of the pilasters of neo-classical architecture. A broad, slightly sculpted band runs along the top and a plain granite face, the height of the front entranceway, along the bottom, with opaque glass brick window openings. The polished black granite lends weight to the light terrazzo upper two storeys of the building. At 100th Street and 102nd Avenue, the building corner is shaved off, presenting passersby with a clean, restrained decorative face, a classical winged figure over the entry, holding cable in one hand and a lightning bolt over his head in the other.[23] It still stands today, partly defining the southern border of Churchill Square.

As City Architect, Dad's responsibilities increased substantially. It's possible this may have played a role in bringing on his first heart attack, but he appeared otherwise to have boundless energy. He played a leading role in encouraging the city to establish a planning department. Without one, the potential for a repetition of the chaos of early twentieth century urban development was considerable in the oil-driven boom years of postwar Alberta. The city needed to anticipate new roads, parks, playgrounds, and shopping centres as the economy grew. By the time he left the city in 1949, a city planner had been appointed.[24] He also pursued the idea of developing a city square that would serve as a nucleus around which buildings, such as a civic auditorium, would be constructed, and which would keep alive the ancient communitarian ideal of civic sociability in a time of rapid expansion.[25] The plan failed to get the approval of the required two-thirds of the city's ratepayers, and the idea languished, coming to life periodically until he made it part of his proposal for the new city hall.

He also became more actively involved in his profession, becoming president of the Alberta Association of Architects. This gave him both a perch from which he could observe developments beyond the city and (mixing metaphors) a pulpit from which to spread his ideas about planning and design. In one of his presidential addresses, he expressed his dismay with the "rows and rows of stereotype houses" that appeared during the war and after: "Surely a small sacrifice in time and money for variety of design would be welcomed by the citizens of everywhere." It did not help that the Central Mortgage and Housing Corporation had decided against using architects in the production of plans for inexpensive homes.[26] In his capacity as president of the AAA (and perhaps also as city architect), he was appointed to serve on a national committee of the Dominion Fire Commissioners to draft legislation regulating hotel, apartment, and rooming house construction, and on a committee of the National Research Council to develop technical requirements for the national building code. He was good at tasks like this. One of the things Cecil Burgess wrote in his obituary was that one could disagree with my father and he would not take it personally; instead, he focused on the issue at hand.

Among the more interesting actions he took as City Architect was the hiring of Jean Wallbridge and Mary Imrie. Wallbridge, as I've mentioned, was a graduate of the U of A architecture program, while Imrie enrolled in it just before the program closed and completed her studies at the University of Toronto. They may have first met at Rule Wynn and Rule, where both worked in the early 1940s, but they really began their careers together in the city architect's office in 1946. They were architects, but they were hired as draughtsmen, an indication of the obstacles women faced in a profession that was very male-centred. In 1947, my father recommended they be granted leave to travel in Europe to study postwar construction and urban planning. Commissioner Dudley Menzies agreed but wondered what it said about office operations if two of the staff could be released when there was so much work to be done. They came back full of ideas and enthusiasm, and Dad put their names forward for reclassification two years later, Wallbridge to become "Technical Assistant in Town Planning" and Imrie "Junior Architect," with commensurate increases in their salaries. "Both these girls," he wrote, "being registered architects, are much more valuable to this department than would be a draughtsman who would accept a salary of this amount. I can assure you it would be next to impossible to replace them with experienced draughtsmen in this salary bracket."[27] This time, Menzies turned down the request. "The Girls," as they came to be known in architectural circles, resigned and went off on further travels, this time by car to South America. It seems they both had inherited money, which gave them a measure of freedom.

When they returned, however, my father had left the city for private practice, and they also decided to strike out on their own, forming the first female architectural partnership in Canada. For the next thirty years they designed many houses and apartment buildings in Edmonton, partly because that was their interest, and partly because, like female doctors practising family medicine and obstetrics, this was the kind of work to which women architects found themselves confined. They continued to maintain personal and professional ties with my father and, after he died, my mother and I paid them a visit at their combined home and office, "Six Acres," overlooking the North Saskatchewan River in the west of the city. It was like a house in the country, both cozy inside and open to the woods around it and the view beyond. They were clearly partners in more than architectural practice, at a time when such relationships were kept quiet, perhaps one reason for the house's somewhat remote location. There was nothing quiet about their personalities, though. We spent part of the afternoon playing "Pit," a card game based on the commodities market, of which I remember little except that it involved a lot of shouting and shrieking in the placing of bids—Barley! Corn! Sugar!—I think with the purpose of drowning out one's opponents as well as collecting cards. They were lots of fun.

In the sometimes small world of my discoveries, I later learned that the two women had designed a house for the parents of another of my carpool friends, Peter Ward. They were the kind of clients Wallbridge and Imrie would have liked. Jean Ward was a potter, and her studio was made a focal point of the house (kiln in the garage). By the same token, the architects were ideal for Peter's parents: "I didn't want any hotshot architect telling me what I wanted," Mrs. Ward told historian Erna Dominey. "There weren't any conflicts with them, they listened and they advised … and I was amazed at how they could produce a house that pleased us so well with so little instruction."[28] Domestic architecture may have been something of a ghetto, but Wallbridge and Imrie were very good at it, making a virtue of what other (male) architects thought was a pain in the neck—the intricate requirements of homeowners and the patience needed to fulfill them. The two women became friends of the Wards, and Peter remembers an evening similar to the day I had spent with them as a young boy, only with the laughter aided by liberal amounts of scotch.

The responsibilities of the city architect's office led to another of my father's prominent buildings, Victoria Composite High School (now Victoria School of the Arts), on which he started work in 1949, but which was not completed until 1951 because of postwar steel shortages. It was the first high school in Edmonton that combined academic, vocational, and technical programs—hence, "composite." It was the kind of newfangled educational idea that got under the skin of traditionalists like Hilda Neatby. Designed in a distinctly modern mode, marked by the flat roofs and clean horizontal massing of its components, and broken by the vertical mass of the school auditorium, it has been described by historians David Murray and Marianne Fedori as "one of the finest buildings [in Edmonton] from the 1940s."[29] In recognition, my father received one of five awards for outstanding schools in North America presented by the American School Publishing Corporation in 1952.

In 1949, he left the city architect's office and went into private practice. Apparently most of his staff followed him. If this was intended to slow the pace of his life or reduce his responsibilities following his first heart attack, however, it didn't do the trick. He was soon very busy, first in Dewar Cawston and Stevenson (1949–51), then in Dewar Stevenson and Stanley (1951–55). At the same time, he didn't do himself any favours. At the time of the unveiling of the city hall design a few years later, he was interviewed by Art Evans, a columnist with the Calgary *Albertan* and an old-style newspaperman (fedora perched on the back of his head) with a droll sense of humour. He described my father as a "fast moving Scotsman who likes wine shirts, yellow ties and ten cigars a day." My father was supposedly off the cigars because of a wager, but would be back on them "after he has picked up his winnings." Evans played several variations on the theme, as he reported on the city hall design—noting in passing about Victoria Composite that "The Little Red School House would be lost in one of its broom closets"—and concluded by remarking that Dewar looked better than he had expected, given the hours he had been putting in: "He sleeps well, eats wells (steaks mostly) and plays snooker and poker for relaxation." He had given up badminton and tennis but hadn't yet been reduced to lawn bowling.[30] One can't help being amused, even now. Nevertheless, one also can't help thinking that, whatever else one can say about the 1950s, the work and social habits of the time left something to be desired for physical well-being.

He continued to explore a modernist vocabulary in his buildings. One of the first was the Biological Sciences Building at the University of Alberta, renamed the Agriculture Building before it was finished. For neither the first time nor the last, his proposed design ran into controversy because of its radically modernist nature. One professor on the advisory committee overseeing the project said it "looked like a door-hinge factory." Changes had to be made, but when construction bids came in for a revised design they were over the original estimated cost. The advisory committee recommended acceptance, but now the government balked, requiring a reduction of size and the elimination of certain features. The building wasn't opened until the fall of 1954.[31] Another of his firm's early projects was the Edmonton Exhibition Grandstand, across Borden Park from our old house, where the horse races were run and the splashy evening shows—singers, dancing girls—were staged during the Exhibition.[32] Others included a new St. Stephen's College building on the U of A campus (very different from the old), the Royal Trust Company building on Jasper Avenue, which helped to change the face of downtown, and Avonmore United Church, as radical, in its way, as the plan for the Biological Sciences building. Sadly, the church later burned to the ground.

As a result of these experiences, my father knew what he was getting into when he put forward his plan for the city hall. Talk of a new building, and of a civic square, had been going on intermittently since the war. Finally, in 1953, it was decided to hold a competition, but this turned out to be more complicated than expected and local architectural firms were invited to make proposals to city council. It was this process that resulted in the selection of Dewar Stevenson and Stanley in November 1953. A month later, my father presented preliminary sketches and a rough model of the proposed building to council, along with a memorandum setting out the principles of design. The building, first of all, was to be "the number one show place" of the city, reflecting the character of "a young and growing province." Since a decision had not yet been made about a civic square, this was to be incorporated into the plan, with the city hall on its north side, dominant, yet part of a "sculptural group" of future buildings. "Functional efficiency" was the goal for both the building itself and the larger civic centre, with attention paid to car parking—"in this automobile age"—and public transportation connections. Aesthetically, the plan sought to "break from the traditional concept of a City Hall where monumentality appears to be the major consideration," and instead to be more in keeping with its time. Mass, materials, and details could achieve their own monumentality, if properly coordinated, yet also serve the end of "economical and efficient function."[33]

What was emerging was a design in the International Style, associated with Henry Russell Hitchcock and Philip Johnson in the United States, Le Corbusier in France, and the Bauhaus in Germany (at least until its leading figures fled Nazi rule in the 1930s).[34] Really more an approach than a style, it was one of the modern movements in architecture that liberated its followers from convention, particularly from the idea that particular building types should follow historical precedents in a way that announced their purpose. In its place, the International Style emphasized truth to materials, a rejection of superfluous (that is, inefficient) ornamentation, and a marriage of form and function. As if to confirm that these were the lines along which he was thinking, my father asked Mayor Hawrelak to authorize funds for Hugh Seton and himself to travel to New York from Montreal, where they would both be attending the annual meeting of the Royal Architectural Institute of Canada in May 1954. They wished to inspect the stunning new United Nations headquarters building, which had been completed two years earlier, and which had included Le Corbusier and the Brazilian modernist Oscar Niemeyer among its consulting architects. There was also a new type of Westinghouse elevator he wanted to consider, which had not yet been installed in Canada. Hawrelak approved the expenditure but, in the end, Seton went to New York on his own. The trip shows that the city hall design continued to evolve after the unveiling, and its influence is evident in the final form of the city council chambers, which stood separate from the main building block to draw special attention to the legislative function of city government.[35]

The chambers component had drawn particular criticism in the plan revealed at the beginning of April, dubbed by some a "grand piano" and by others a "casket." As a result of the subsequent New York trip, it was streamlined in imitation of the portion of the UN building that housed the General Assembly and Security Council, though it continued to be commonly described as "swank." Anticipating controversy, my father had said at the unveiling, "We're in for some awful blasts," but he was still taken aback by their force. "Tell Architect Dewar to change his brand of whiskey," one anonymous critic wrote to the *Journal*, presumably referring to the popular scotch label, "Dewar's." More disturbing than the letters was the *Journal's* own editorial deriding the "Nightmare In City Square," and referring sarcastically to Lewis Carroll's *Through the Looking Glass* in search of apposite phrases. This forced my father to respond, which he did in a speech to the Gyro Club. He gave a brief outline of the history of architecture and stressed, perhaps wisely, the prohibitive cost of the kind of ornate structure common in the past, though he also said that the design purposely envisioned a building "with clean lines and 'no gargoyles' on the corners," and that city council had agreed. The tone of the letters to the *Journal* grew more positive and city council members, who cannot have been too surprised by the design presented to them, gave their stamp of approval before the end of April.[36]

The impression created by the building that eventually resulted was one of lightness, rather than monumentality. This was achieved partly by concealing the structural skeleton behind alternating bands of windows and ivory-coloured marble running the full width of the building, and partly by diminishing the mass of the central administrative block by pinching the ends of its basic rectangular shape to form a kind of elongated lozenge. The area of the windowless end walls was in this way reduced, while the north and south faces angled slightly inward from the central axis. Horizontal aluminum louvres on the southern exposure provided shade from direct sunlight and heightened the illusion of weightlessness.[37] A second component, in addition to the council chambers that extended from the second floor over the plaza in front of the main office block, was a unit containing public services that projected outward at ground level for ease of access. Few buildings of the time so successfully deployed the ideas and devices of international modernism. In the catalogue of a show mounted in 2007 at the Art Gallery of Alberta called "Capital Modern," surveying Edmonton architecture from the 1930s to the 1960s, Trevor Boddy, the historian who had got my dander up enough to set me off on my researches in the first place, compiled a list of what he considered the best buildings of each decade of the period the show covered. I was pleased to note that the building he chose for the 1950s was the city hall.[38]

As a result of my investigations into the origins of the city hall design, I developed a series of lectures on the history of architecture for a course in the social and cultural history of Canada that I taught at Mount Saint Vincent University. The series extended from rural domestic housing in New France to native houses on the northwest coast to Georgian classicism in late eighteenth-century Upper Canada, and on to neo-Gothic architecture in Ontario (in which I had long been interested because of the work of William Westfall on churches), and the chateau style of railway hotels in the early twentieth century, including (of course) the Banff Springs. The final lecture was on the International Style, and incorporated the city hall as an example. The view of the history of architecture that I passed on to my students was informed by my own past.

Teenage Ken in backyard of house on 112 Avenue S.

Chapter Three
Camping and Character

When we moved back to the Highlands in 1956, I returned to Cromdale school, entering Grade 6. Before long, I was moved forward into Grade 7, "skipping" a grade, in the lingo of the time. I was certainly a good student academically, but I doubt whether the same thing would have happened if we had stayed on the south side. The teachers in Windsor Park School hadn't known me as well as those at Cromdale, where I had received honours marks from the beginning. There are actual marks on my report card, even for Grade 1: "H" (Excellent) in both oral and silent reading, "A" (Very Good) in oral and written language, "H" in arithmetic, "B" (Good) in art, and so on. This, especially the "B" in art ("creativeness and skill"), established something of a pattern. Under General Comments, my teacher, Miss Brown, wrote, "Kenneth has had perfect attendance for the school year" ("perfect" underlined twice), and in the concluding portion regarding my promotion to Grade 2 she noted that I had "passed with 'Honors.'" Does anyone pass Grade 1 with honours anymore?

I'm not sure skipping was entirely a good thing, but it's pretty difficult to construct a counterfactual history of my schooling (much less my life) on the basis of my "acceleration" not having happened. My first report in Grade 7 showed some of my marks to be below the class average and three (circled in red) to be failures. Mr. Laube, my teacher, noted that my marks were "not up to what I know he can do," because of my late arrival. They remained stable or improved through the rest of the year, but I still finished the year with only a "Pass." They continued to improve the next year and I returned to an honours standing, but I remember feeling a little out of place socially. It probably didn't help that I was twelve years old while my classmates were thirteen and maturing ahead of me. My Grade 8 class was pretty unruly and poor Mr. Johnston, a quiet man (and the school principal), had some trouble keeping order. He gave me the strap once for throwing chalk while he was working at the board, with his back to the classroom. I wasn't the only guilty party, but I was the one who was caught when he whipped around to see what was going on. I think this may have upped my status in certain circles and helped in my efforts to fit in.

The question of just where I fit was confused by the fact that some of my out-of-school activities were more strictly age-related. I had played hockey for the Cromdale Mites, for example, since 1953, except for the year we lived on the south side. I have team pictures for every year because we had won successive Community League championships, and I can see myself growing older in each one. By 1956–57, my Grade 8 year, I was beginning to stretch up from the chubby little kid of earlier years, but most of my classmates at this point would have moved on to the Bantam league, so I was a little out of sync. I don't recall this bothering me until a couple of years later, when I was in Grade 10 and still playing Bantam, while others had moved on to Midget. At a practice held in the Edmonton Gardens at the beginning of the season, I was embarrassed—mortified might be a better word—to notice two girls from Eastglen High School sitting in the stands across the rink from our bench. I think it was Pat Overton and Bunny McLean, popular girls a year or two ahead of me. They had noticed me on the ice and seemed to be talking about me. I was sure they were remarking on what my age had to be. When I left the team and dropped out of organized hockey not long afterward, it was not because of this encounter, but because I didn't think my skills were any longer up to the mark. Nevertheless, I was clearly self-conscious about my age.

Cromdale stopped at Grade 8 and I changed schools for Grade 9, walking about fifteen blocks east along 112th Avenue to Highlands Junior High. Here, and at Eastglen, where I went the following year for Grade 10, there began a perceptible new phase of my life, not just for the obvious reasons associated with the onset of puberty and adolescence, but because my circle of friends widened and I became active in numerous clubs, both in and out of school. While still at Highlands, I became part of a band, in which I played the drums, of all things. I had taken piano lessons earlier, before we moved to the south side, but hadn't returned to them when we moved back. Instead, I had briefly played the trumpet before taking up the drums. I think this inconstancy reflected a basic shortage of musical talent. The drums lasted longer than either of the other instruments—long enough for me to become a fan of Gene Krupa and Buddy Rich, leading jazz drummers of the time. They also got me on stage, playing with the band in school "lits" (short for literary society), most memorably Buddy Holly's "That'll Be the Day." Talent or not, I must have enjoyed being on stage, since I later joined with Woody Johnson and Peter Ward, whom I first met at Highlands, to form the Eastglen Trio, and we performed at various school events, singing songs then being made popular by the Kingston Trio—"Tom Dooley," "The Tatooed Lady," "Sloop John B," and others. Peter provided instrumental accompaniment on his ukelele.

I got on stage again in Grade 10 as a member of the cast of "Cloud Seven," a comedy written by the American playwright Max Wilk that the drama department put on. I played Russ, the "dashing" boyfriend of Sally Reece, who was the daughter of the lead character, and who was played by Doreen Meisner, a girl in Grade 11. Our parts required us to kiss in the half-open front door of the Reece home, upstage from the audience. This was quite risqué for all concerned. I also became involved in the school newspaper, the *Eastglen Gazette*, and joined the badminton and ping pong clubs, and the Booster Club. The purpose of the last was to cultivate school spirit, which entailed cheerleading at inter-school sports events and promotion of good works of one kind and another. The student body was divided into "houses" and somehow I became a member of the House Two executive. In short, I became much more outgoing than I had been previously—downright bright-eyed and bushy-tailed, and not a James Dean figure at all, though Dean represented a kind of transgressive ideal to most of us. By the end of the year I was standing for vice-president of the Students' Union, and I won, at least in part because of the amusing speech I gave, much of which I cribbed from a speech my brother Bob had given for a similar purpose when he was in Grade 9.

Thus began my career in student politics and my involvement in teen organizations across the city. One of these was directly related to school, the Council of High School Presidents and Vice-Presidents, of which I became a member *ex-officio*, both in Grade 11 and Grade 12, when I became Students' Union president and council chairman (no use of gender-neutral terms in those days). I can't recall what all we did, but I do remember our collective amusement when Sue Peers, the vice-president from Ross Sheppard High School, explained to Mr. Innes, the council advisor and principal of Strathcona, that the way to get one's jeans to the required tightness of fit was to sit in a bathtub of steaming hot water, then allow them to dry while one still had them on. Mr. Innes's amusement was clearly mixed with astonishment.

Similarly, my memory is poor on the details of the United Nations Association Seminar at the Banff School of Fine Arts that I attended in the summer of 1960, having won a scholarship for achievement in Grade 11 Social Studies, a course that was a hodgepodge of history and other subjects. I had also competed in a public speaking contest under the tutelage of George Brown, one of our teachers and an organizer of the seminar. My topic had been the condition of refugees in postwar Europe and the efforts of the UN High Commission for Refugees to assist them. Though I lost the contest, this aroused my interest in the UN. If the details are vague, I have a strong sense of the seminar's general seriousness of purpose. We heard lectures on science as an international enterprise, world population growth, comparative cultures, and the French Fifth Republic, which had emerged in 1958 and brought Charles de Gaulle to the presidency. The last of these was given by W. J. Eccles, whom I later encountered as a professor at the University of Alberta. I am certain about the topics only because I still have a copy of the program.

What I remember without any aid is the song composed by Bill Hrychuk, later president of the Strathcona Students' Union, in response to a challenge from the girls at the seminar to the boys. It was a variation on the well-known ditty (sung to the tune of Antonín Dvořák's

Humoresque No. 7) that began, "Passengers will please refrain / From flushing toilets while the train / Is standing in the station, I love you." I remember Bill's lyrics in their entirety: "Will you ladies please refrain / From shouting challenges insane / While shutting out the mountains and the view; / We will smite you down with thunder / For your disrespectful blunder / We can keep our heads, so why can't you." So, I infer, do our memories work, or perhaps it's only mine. Sadly, Bill died prematurely in 1981, as I have since learned. The Religious and Moral Education Council of the Alberta Teachers' Association subsequently created the William D. Hrychuk Memorial Award, which it gives to one of its members for outstanding achievement.[39]

The common thread in these activities was a kind of innocent earnestness and sobriety, not at all uncommon in the 1950s. Even activities that otherwise seem frivolous in retrospect had an element of social concern, and sometimes a touch of self-importance. Many years later I had a conversation with an anthropologist friend in which, for some reason, we got to talking about our respective religious backgrounds. I said mine was Presbyterian, shading over time into intermittent United Church attendance. In Canada, of course, most Presbyterians had joined in forming the United Church at the time of church union in 1925, and this may have explained my parents' church affiliation, to the extent that they had one by the time I came along. I attended Sunday School as a child, though not very regularly, and belonged to a United Church young people's group for a time as a teenager. My anthropologist friend was pretty foursquare about the difference between Roman Catholics and Presbyterians. Catholics, she said, were burdened by a sense of guilt, while the Presbyterian (perhaps Protestant) counterpart was a sense of duty. This was an idea based on Max Weber's theory about the connection between Protestantism and the rise of capitalism, about which I was sceptical in historical terms, but I had never thought about its application to myself before. There was no doubt that I had been drawn into many activities, and into some kind of leadership role, partly out of a sense of duty.

Another of these activities was a teen club called Club Stardust, whose main activity, and reason for being, was holding weekly dances in the Highlands Community Hall, near Highlands Junior High. We always hired a band, usually Wes Dakus and the Rebels, who had a twangy guitar sound and played mostly instrumental music. Wes hailed from Mannville, east of Edmonton, and the Rebels were the most popular rock 'n' roll band in town, eventually gaining a provincial, then a national, reputation. They were so clean-cut: white shirts, narrow ties, closely cut suits, polished shoes, pompadour haircuts. When Wes died in 2013, the Toronto *Globe and Mail* published a full-length obituary, nicely evoking his career, though the headline was slightly misleading in referring to him as "Edmonton's answer to Elvis." Wes was certainly the local king of rock 'n' roll, but there was little that was controversial about him, as was evident in the comment of someone from the Canadian National Exhibition when the band played there in the 1960s: "They're really a fine bunch of boys and they've been averaging pretty well sellouts," the man said.[40] A fine bunch of boys, indeed. They were always very cool on stage, no histrionics and no swivelling hips, while on the gym floor scores of teenagers jived the night away. They played the odd waltz, especially toward the end, couples dancing closely. I spent many Friday nights at Stardust, working the admissions table, cleaning up, and dancing myself, though the girl I was most interested in already had a boyfriend.

Even Stardust had its dutiful side. We joined with other clubs in a city-wide organization that became a money-raising vehicle for good causes, one of them being the "Shower of Silver" campaign, which involved collecting coins in glass milk bottles provided by local dairies. It was still possible at the time to have one's milk delivered by "the milkman," who drove his truck from door to door, delivering bottled milk and collecting empties. A few years earlier, he had done this by horse-drawn milk wagon, which always stirred a little excitement when it clip-clopped down the street, leaving droppings in its wake. Proceeds from the campaign, meagre as they were, went to the Red Feather campaign of the Community Chest, forerunner of the United Way.

Stardust also led me into the Miss Edmonteen Ball Association, whose purpose was summed up in the name. Pat Overton, one of the girls whose presence embarrassed me at my last Bantam practice, was

Miss Edmonteen in my Grade 10 year. The following year, when I was among the organizers, a girl named Gwen Guthrie (from Ross Sheppard) won, and a bunch of us went to the Western Canada Teen Conference, held that year in Ponoka, a town about an hour's drive south of Edmonton. One purpose of the conference was to choose a Western Canada Teen Queen, which is a little embarrassing to write down on paper today. There were also speakers and panel discussions, at least one of which said as much about the time as the queen competition. It was on the subject of potential careers and, according to the *Edmonton Journal* report, girls attending the panel asked one of the members if he thought "any post–high school training was important for a girl who planned a career as a housewife." The panelist, who was the supervisor of guidance counselling in the provincial department of education, replied that it was good "insurance," especially if something should happen to your husband and you found it necessary to support yourself.[41] These were the days in which it was often said of young women attending university that their goal was an MRS. degree, a joke that was dead within a decade. At the conference, it turned out that the judges choosing the teen queen also had the job of selecting the "outstanding teen-ager" from the fifteen clubs attending, and I was put forward as the Edmonton candidate. I don't know if there had been any previous selection process elsewhere, but there had certainly been none in our case. In any event, I was chosen, stealing some of the limelight from Gwen, who came in third in the queen contest.

Cheesy though all of this seems in retrospect, I felt good about it at the time. I don't think it went to my head, if only because Woody's mocking intonation of my new title always kept things in perspective. I have more difficulty looking back at the Eastglen "Blue and Gold" Year Book for my graduating year. The year book itself was very nicely put together. Peter was the editor and Woody the advertising manager. John Lewis, one of another circle of friends, was the compositing editor and designer, and he must have had a lot to do with creating its stylish look. Not surprisingly, memory was a recurring theme, from Principal Stanley Deane's opening wish that graduates take good memories of Eastglen with them into the future, to Peter's definition of a year book as the carrier and trigger of those memories, to my own "Class History," which looked forward to a future when we would reminisce about "our school days," and on through other items.

This is standard fare for year books, whose purpose, as Peter wrote, is the making of memories. Men and women have always remembered, in one way or another, but how and what we remember is governed by culture. In modern times, for a culture that many think is losing its sense of history, it is striking just how many sites and modes of memory we have, from individual autobiography and memoir, to family photograph albums, to private anniversaries and public commemorations of past events. I think the roots of modern remembering lie in the Victorian era, when it became customary to do things—such as taking photographs and keeping diaries—whose express purpose was remembering in the future. Year books exist on this spectrum of memory creation. In the case of my own from 1961, it evokes many warm memories, as was its purpose, but they are hard to separate from the cringing feeling I have when I read my "President's Message," in which I quoted Dale Carnegie—he of *How to Win Friends and Influence People* fame—on the importance of smiling in human relations. Now *that* was cheesy.

* * * * * *

I worked part-time at a couple of different jobs when I was going to school. When we lived on the south side, I sold magazine subscriptions door-to-door in our neighbourhood, having been recruited for the job by someone who had shown up at Windsor Park school. Compensation took the form of points that could be redeemed for products, like Air Miles. I didn't last very long. After we returned to the Highlands, a friend and I cleaned up the lot at the local Burger King Drive-In every day after school for a couple of years. It was owned by Jim Rae and Bill Jarvis, two local men who pioneered the drive-in restaurant business in Edmonton, eventually adding Kentucky Fried Chicken to their menu, under franchise, and growing to become a small chain. They both had day jobs at Imperial Oil, but they often dropped by to check

Child of the Fifties

on operations, do odd jobs, and make sure everyone on site was doing theirs, which they did with genial good humour. When the American Burger King chain expanded into Canada, it had to acquire the Canadian rights to the name from Jim and Bill, which must have earned them a tidy sum, though they retained rights to northern Alberta until 1995.[42] My friend's and my job was to pick up all the garbage that customers threw from their car windows onto the ground instead of into the garbage containers located just beyond their front bumpers. We entertained ourselves by placing the small clear plastic ketchup containers that accompanied the french fries onto the railway tracks that ran by the lot, gratified by the squirts of viscous red liquid when a train rolled by. Our bonus was free milk shakes and burgers that the women inside gave us, depending on their mood. Later, in high school—it must have been after I turned sixteen—I worked briefly at Woodward's Department Store on Thursday nights (shopping night) and Saturdays, in the butcher's department and in men's wear.

My first summer job was at Camp Keewaydhin, the YMCA boys' camp on Lake Wabamun, west of the city on the road to Jasper. The Y had operated a boys' camp in different locations more or less continuously since 1907, but during the Second World War it became a project of the Y's Men's Club, which was re-established in 1943 after earlier failures.[43] My father was the club's first president, and he was very much involved in the purchase, the following year, of the new camp property at Wabamun, on Jackfish Bay. He surveyed the site and designed the original dining hall and cabins, which were built by work parties of Y's Men who drove out from Edmonton on weekends. Eventually these ventures included an annual Sunday gathering that included wives and children. While the men worked on construction, upkeep, and repairs, the women—the Y's Menettes—looked after the children and provided a picnic for everyone at midday. Someone organized games and competitions in a large playing field just inside the entrance—three-legged races, relays, tug-of-war. These "Family Days" were my first introduction to the camp. After my father died, I occasionally visited the Y in the city for swimming and table tennis, but I only went to Keewaydhin once as an ordinary camper.

I began working as a counsellor one year and then graduated to more senior positions—waterfront director, program director, assistant camp director. These jobs became one focal point of my adolescence, providing opportunities for enjoyment, as well as a modest income, and for initiation into adult responsibilities. I think they came to me, in part, as a form of patronage, since some of the people who ran the camp, including Harold Sprague, who chaired the camp's board of directors for a couple of the years I worked there, had been friends of my father and regarded me in a semi-paternal sort of way. In a moment revealing of the time, Harold once took me to lunch at the Royal Glenora Country Club, in the river valley up from the High Level Bridge. When the waiter asked me what I would like to drink, I hesitated, never having had "a drink" at lunch before, and replied, "Scotch." This prompted Harold to launch into a lesson on midday cocktails, recommending (as I recall) a Manhattan. I don't think it registered that this was just the kind of lunch that my father would often have had. Harold also gave me work helping with deliveries from his furniture store on 109th Street. At the same time, I had become a qualified life guard and swimming instructor through the programs of the Red Cross and the Royal Life Saving Society, which doubtless also helped to get me the job at camp. I learned canoeing on the job.

Camps ran for two-week periods, nothing like the four and eight weeks common in many Ontario camps of the day, both private and those run by the YMCA and other organizations. Those camps, many of them dating back to the early twentieth century, were nevertheless the model on which we operated. The campers ranged in age from 8 or 9 years old to 15 or 16. The younger boys stayed in cabins, the older ones in tents mounted on wooden floors, each unit supervised by a counsellor. There were counsellors-in-training (CITs), as well as a cook (Cap Fuhr for most of my time), a caretaker, a nurse, and the "senior staff" (waterfront and program directors, sometimes assistants, and the camp director). In addition to the cabins and the dining hall, there was now a recreation hall (linked to the dining hall, forming an "L"), a craft hall, an infirmary, and cabins for most of the senior staff. All of these were painted in a warm brown colour, similar to the colour used in national parks, somehow evocative of rusticity and nature. On the waterfront, there was a large H-shaped pier, a diving raft, canoe racks, and a small building for paddles, oars, and life jackets that we called "The Rudder Inn." There was also a rudimentary chapel in the woods—a fenced-in area with benches and a cross—located on a path that ran out onto the point of the 33-acre property.

At the heart of the camp's activities and organization was the idea that "going back to nature" and "roughing it" was an experience that was educational in the widest sense and also somehow renewing. We offered instruction in camp craft, nature craft, archery, and riflery on land, and swimming, boating, and canoeing on water. Out-tripping—overnight hikes and canoe trips on the lake—offered campers a chance to put what they learned into practice and develop (at least, so we thought) their self-reliance and cooperative skills. The way all this was experienced—the imaginary medium through which they returned to nature—was the Indian, or at least an idea of Indian-ness. This was well before the terms native, First Nations, or aboriginal people came into wide use, much less indigenous.

The camp name, Keewaydhin, supposedly meant "northwest wind," though no one ever said in which native language (it was apparently Ojibway). The junior cabins were all named after the six nations of the Iroquois: Seneca, Cayuga, Onondaga, Oneida, Mohawk, and Tuscarora. These were all peoples on the American side of the border, of course, in New York state, many of whom migrated north into southern Ontario after the American Revolution, but their aura was continental in scope. (We were not aware of the Iroquoian term Haudenosuanee.) Once each camp we had a Council Fire, held in a designated area out beyond the chapel on the way to the point. Camp leaders dressed up as Indians, and pseudo-Indian ceremonies were performed, amidst the handing out of awards. One highlight of the camp experience was the "vigil," in which an individual spent three days and two nights in the wild, without equipment, surviving by himself and contemplating nature. An especially embarrassing memory of my camp years—embarrassing at the time, not just in retrospect, as in my quoting Dale Carnegie—was the ceremonial recognition of my own vigil at a Council

Fire, where I was decked out in "Indian" costume, though decked out is perhaps the wrong term, given what little I actually had on. Fortunately, the bonfire was always large, so I wasn't cold. I don't remember the Indian name I was given.

In my last year working for the camp, a new man came to the Y, an African Canadian from the Toronto Y, and he and I got to talking one day about this and that, and the Indian theme of the camp somehow arose. The man said, in none too gentle a manner, that he thought the whole thing was racist. This was the first time anyone had ever suggested to me (I was not yet 21 years old) that anything I was involved in was racist, and I rather balked at the idea, even though he wasn't actually accusing me of *being* a racist. In fact, the term wasn't even in common use in Canada, though it shortly became so. I thought that, far from looking down on "the Indian" and "the Indian way of life," we were holding it up as an ideal.

I was reading a little about the history of camping by then, but it was only later that I learned where this ideal had come from, and how Indians and summer camp came to be linked so closely together. I discovered that the connection had been made early in the twentieth century, and that, if any single person could be said to have been responsible, it was Ernest Thompson Seton (1860–1946), best known as the author of *Wild Animals I Have Known* (1898), a collection of realistic animal stories that Margaret Atwood pointed to in *Survival*, her popular work of literary history, as evidence of a reluctance to humanize animals in Canadian literature.[44] He also wrote *Two Little Savages: Being the Adventures of Two Boys Who Lived as Indians and What They Learned* (1903), a novel in which a boy flees an abusive father by escaping to the bush and living with a friend "like Injuns." This was a story, but it was also a handbook of nature lore and woodcraft for children. It had diagrams of teepees, and instructions on how to sew leather moccasins and make a fire by rubbing sticks together (something I never caught on to, even under the pressure of my vigil). Daniel Francis, whose book *The Imaginary Indian* opened my eyes to the variety of representations of native peoples, observed that it was the only work of fiction he knew that had an index.[45]

Two Little Savages became the founding text of a movement Seton initiated called the League of Woodcraft Indians. Native peoples, in Seton's hands, were held up as a model for North American youth. Far from being drunken, lazy, and dissolute, he said, Indians represented closeness to nature and an appreciation of its wonders. They were spiritual in outlook and communal, even socialistic, in their customs and habits, and they had been free from vice until Europeans arrived, bringing disease, liquor, and greed. The story of contact, he once said, had been "an unbroken narrative of injustice, fraud and robbery."[46] The lesson he preached was that selfish, materialistic, acquisitive White society had much to learn from Indians.

The woodcraft movement spread like wildfire before the First World War. Groups were called tribes (as we later referred to our camper units), leaders were called chiefs (as we called our camp director on "Indian" occasions). It instilled worthy moral precepts—protect the song birds, don't make a dirty camp, play fair—and the programs it implemented were set out in another of Seton's books, *The Birch-bark Roll of the Woodcraft Indians* (1906). Ours were almost identical. A girls' movement was also started, the Camp Fire Girls, and Seton's influence extended to the contemporary Boy Scout movement, begun by Robert Baden-Powell, though the scouts were much less enamoured of Indians and more inclined to emulate a military model rather than Seton's communalism and pacifism. The difference persisted down to my day, at least in my own view of scouting, with all of its badges and its uniforms.

Seton became an inspiration for the camping movement in general, especially through a Toronto YMCA boys' work secretary, Taylor Statten, who directed one of the early Y camps for boys in 1905 and founded his own private camp in Algonquin Park, west of Ottawa, in 1921. Even as a teenager, I knew of Taylor Statten and Camp Ahmek. Many prominent Canadian men spent their boyhood summers there, including (as everyone later learned) Pierre Elliott Trudeau, whose buckskin-clad figure, paddling a canoe by himself on some lonely northern waterway, became an iconic image of the 1970s. "Ahmek" was a name of Indian origin (Ojibway) and Statten was known as "The Chief."

Seton's ideas, of course, did not exist in isolation. The camping movement was a response to rapid industrialization and urbanization, and it was part of a wider movement of moral and social reform in the early decades of the twentieth century, often led by people whose roots lay in the countryside, but who (or whose parents) had moved to the city. The ideal of the simple, natural, healthy life—a life, supposedly, as Indians had led it—had great appeal. This was also the time of the conservation movement and the beginnings of present-day Parks Canada, and when the wilderness paintings of Tom Thomson and the Group of Seven captured a wide audience. New interest in the Group, and in their patron, the Toronto ophthalmologist and enthusiast of "the north," Dr. James M. MacCallum, flourished in the late 1960s under the influence of art historians J. Russell Harper, Dennis Reid, and Peter Mellen, and it was through this revival that I began to better understand the historical continuum on which my camping youth existed. The idea that the wilderness was not pristine, but rather was made, or "constructed," by human beings, grew out of this new awareness of the Group and the sources of their "naturalism" in Scandinavian landscape art and other painting traditions.

More recently, the camping movement itself has become a subject of study by cultural historians, most notably in Canada by Sharon Wall of the University of Winnipeg. Wall's work, and that of her colleagues, is just as challenging in its own way to my idea of camp as was that of the man from Toronto who raised the question of racism. Focusing on camps in Ontario from the First World War to the 1950s, she discusses how their organization and programs were shaped by class, gender, new ideas of childhood and child psychology, and the mythification of native peoples. She argues that camping represented a form of "antimodernism," a rejection of the city and its all-enveloping consumerism, while at the same time its quest for order and efficiency, and its adoption of the methods of progressive education, made it a distinctly modern phenomenon. "Playing Indian" was a "racialized expression of twentieth-century antimodernism," she writes, a colonial (or post-colonial) appropriation of native symbols and rituals for the purpose of allaying discomfort with modern alienation.[47]

Wall uses her organizing concepts in a nuanced way and provides a fascinating account of summer camping, both boys' and girls', in all of its dimensions, but I am sceptical of how much those concepts, especially antimodernism, add to our understanding of the camping experience. There is no doubt that "roughing it" was thought to build character, especially in boys, and to counter the debilitating effects of the soft city life. Speaking to a reporter in 1964 about an upcoming canoe camp on the North Saskatchewan River, George Singleton, the general secretary of the Edmonton Y (that is, the man in charge), said that the experience of canoeing the river would be transforming for the campers: "They won't be the same boys after the trip," he said. "It's a lesson in co-operation and self-reliance."[48] In the same year, a new camp director was appointed, succeeding Grant McKeen, who had held the position for a number of years. His name was Rich Bailey, and he came from Toronto to be Director of Camping and Youth at the Y. Rich was a little taken aback by how primitive the facilities were at Keewaydhin, and particularly by the pit toilets that all the campers used, and by the simple washing shelter down near the lake where everyone performed their ablutions at a long tin-lined sink with four or five taps that provided only cold water from the lake. He proposed that proper washhouses be built, with hot water, showers, and flush toilets. He was quite right, of course, that this would be a big improvement in sanitation, but we all thought the idea contrary to "roughing it," though not all that surprising coming from an effete easterner. Rich went on to hold various senior positions in the Y, including CEO of YMCA Canada.

One could come up with numerous other examples of how camp was an escape from modernity, but they co-existed with many other examples of how camp was no escape at all. Those hardy canoe campers on the North Saskatchewan took advantage of their overnight stop at Drayton Valley to walk into town for pop or a milkshake, and their food *en route* included instant potatoes and canned beans. There were other ways in which camp was actually an agent of modernization. As my interest in camping grew more serious, I read books about camp programming and theory, if theory it was. Pre-eminent in the latter category was *Camping and Character: A Camp Experiment in Charac-*

ter Education, by Hedley S. Dimock and Charles E. Hendry, which had been published in 1929 and quickly became the bible of the camping movement, depositing an overlay of semi-scientific educational theory on Ernest Thompson Seton's mystical primitivism.[49]

The book's foreword was written by William H. Kilpatrick, a professor at Columbia University Teachers' College and a leading proponent of child-centred education. Quotations from the philosopher John Dewey, the father of progressive education, were sprinkled throughout, in chapter epigraphs and in the text. I took on Dimock and Hendry's message pretty thoroughly, writing in my annual Program Director's Report in 1964 that, "The general aim of Camp Keewaydhin is to train young boys in the ability to work and plan together democratically, to develop skills, self-reliance and initiative, and at the same time to provide two weeks of fun within a safe and healthy environment." Their model was Taylor Statten's Ahmek, and they contrasted the naturalness and simplicity of life in the woods with the artificiality and complexity of the civilized city, while at the same time they also had their eye on the demands of modern corporate life for teamwork and leadership.

My reading of Dimock and Hendry, together with the ideas and thinking of other members of staff, led to a change in the structure of camp programming, from a "centralized" program to one that was "decentralized." The centralized program was developed entirely by senior staff and established a rigid schedule for the day, from "wakey and polar bears" (early morning dip) at 7:30 a.m., to "fag bell" (a signal for boys to come to the dining hall to set tables for each unit), "flag raising" (there was a flagpole on the foreground of the dining and recreation halls) and breakfast, cabin cleanup and "tribal duties." Two morning instruction periods followed, then late morning "general swim," and on through lunch (with its own fag bell), siesta, two afternoon instruction periods, and so on until flag lowering at 7:45 p.m. and "planned evening program." Each activity was announced by the ringing of a bell mounted atop the main entrance to the dining and rec halls. Camp was not unlike school in this way.

The decentralized program loosened things up, retaining a basic schedule but allowing for greater flexibility in instructional activities, making it possible for units to plan their own schedules—"democratically," I explained in my annual report—and even to change their eating times as long as they gave the kitchen advance notice. "The curriculum," wrote Dimock and Hendry, who thought of camp life as a curriculum and a model of what school *ought* to be like, "cannot and should not be created in advance."[50] Like other aspects of progressive theory, this placed a lot of responsibility on the staff closest to the activity in question (the counsellors in our case) and often resulted in "democratic" decisions being made along lines they planned for originally, though it was also true that our revised structure was a halfway measure, limited by our resources and our caution.

Wall is quite aware of these contradictions, which is why she stresses the "ambivalence" of camping in its relation to modernity. She goes so far as to ask, in the title of her conclusion, "All Antimodern Melts into Modern?" It is a good question, since any ambivalence that existed at Keewaydhin about "questions of escapism, isolation, wilderness, and roughing it" had little element of intellectual or cultural conflict about it. It had more to do with things like fatigue or bad company. As she notes herself, the antimodernism of summer camping was only skin deep; far from being distressed, or even unhappy about modernity, "camp enthusiasts … were active optimists animated by the promise of therapeutic recreation."[51] If the lessons I took from Dimock and Hendry at the time mean anything—or even my quoting of Dale Carnegie, for that matter—they mean that this statement describes my own approach to camping, no matter how much I was taken by the rising of the moon in the evening, or the glow of the campfire, or the sound of coyotes in the distance. I noted all of those things in the journals I kept of canoe trips on the North Saskatchewan.

The concept of cultural appropriation is another matter, though even here I have some hesitations. Campers did not only play Indian; they also played Vikings (a "Viking Funeral," complete with roaring bonfire on a floating raft just offshore, *away* from the pier), Klondike gold prospectors (in a kind of treasure hunt game), and Voyageurs. Those canoe trips on the river were Voyageur Camp, and they were something of a capstone of the Keewaydhin camping experience. A recurring topic of discussions about camp programming was how to keep activities interesting enough to draw boys back for more in the following year. There were things one could do at the residence camp—introducing more variety, offering opportunities to improve skills—but there were also other camps that offered a different experience altogether. For a couple of years we put on horseback-riding camps at Jasper, where we could stay at the YMCA holiday camp at Lake Edith, not far from Jasper Park Lodge. The one we offered year after year was Voyageurs, which had the advantage not only of building on the skills in canoeing and swimming acquired at the residence camp but of the excitement of riding a few rapids and camping in something close to genuine wilderness, at least some of the time.

Usually, Voyageurs lasted for a week or ten days, starting with a few days of preparation at Wabamun—in practice, many boys registered who had not been to Camp Keewaydhin—followed by a week on the river, canoeing from Rocky Mountain House to Edmonton. These trips were in self-conscious emulation of the "rivermen of old" travelling between the historic fur trading posts of Rocky and Fort Edmonton. I'm not sure that they were as life-transforming as George Singleton predicted, but they certainly were demanding. The first trip that I recall—it may have been the first I took—was in 1961, and it started off very badly. Of the eleven canoes on the trip (with eighteen campers and four staff), three tipped early on the first day. My journal notes that the atmosphere as we left had been a little too carefree, but this may have been a retrospective judgment.

Two of the canoes got to shore and righted themselves at the cost only of wet gear. The third had a staff member in the stern, and another staff member stayed behind to help. When they did not show up by nightfall at the campsite we had made, the camp leader, Grant McKeen, and I returned to Rocky Mountain House the next morning, having found a farmer who was willing to drive us back with a canoe. When we made our way down river, we soon found a canoe overturned and wedged in a tree fallen in the river. We managed to get to it, tie up, and get ourselves into the swiftly flowing water to investigate. The canoe had split just behind the bow seat, but we were able to pry

Child of the Fifties

it loose and retrieve most of the gear and food supplies before heading off in hopes of finding the two staff members and two campers. By this time, having started out nervously, we were becoming frantic. When we found their campsite, containing a note saying they had hiked back to Rocky, our mood changed from frantic to annoyed. In the end, we were reunited, with the loss of only a canoe and one day of the trip. Everyone became a little more serious.

The year in which we broke our routine—ambition getting the better of someone—was 1963, when we started from the Tomahawk ferry, a day-and-a-half's paddling upriver of Edmonton, and travelled to Prince Albert, Saskatchewan. It was a much longer trip than usual, lasting over two weeks on the river, and we had a larger camp, with thirty boys and three leaders in fifteen canoes. Grant, the director, fell ill just before we came into the city, which left me and Kofi Amankwah, a Ghanaian who was studying medicine at the University of Alberta, as the only staff. It was a good thing that Kofi was as cheerful and adaptable as he was, and that we got along well together.

The trip felt even longer than it was. The North Saskatchewan below Edmonton slows down and widens, with frequent long straight stretches and numerous islands and sandbars, the more so as one moves across the Saskatchewan border. A recent book by Edmonton writer Myrna Kostash, *Reading the River*, tells the history of the waterway and its users in a kind of anthology of writings by explorers, traders, novelists, and poets.[52] It might have made things more interesting for us in 1963, though it's more a view from the banks than from the river itself. We traced our progress by the successive ferries we passed—Bruderheim, Waskatenau, Myrnam, Maidstone, and so on—most of which no longer exist. Bridges were also markers: Shandro, Brosseau, and others. In other words, this was not really a wilderness adventure, though it had its own challenges. Caragana bushes offered little shelter from the hailstones that poured down on us one day, freezing the ground on which we stood in bare feet, and the slowness of the river made for long days of hard paddling to make our schedule. We had been sent off from Edmonton by Mayor Elmer Roper, bearing letters from him to the mayors of North Battleford and Prince Albert, and there were plans for official greeting parties at both cities. Despite our best efforts, we were a day late getting into Battleford, though we managed Prince Albert on time.

Like other aspects of Voyageur camp, the mayor's letters also harkened back to the days of the fur trade, when the river was the major communication route, and on this trip we organized the camp into groups named after famous traders: Peter Pond, David Thompson, Simon Fraser and Alexander Mackenzie. Still, among the highlights was the sighting of a small airplane on the morning of the day we were to arrive in Battleford, from which a can dropped with a note in it to give us an estimate of the remaining distance. Harold Sprague and another board member, Stu Dewar (no relation), had come from Edmonton to offer us encouragement and had rented the plane (and hired a pilot) in Battleford. We were warmly welcomed on our arrival, as we were later in P.A. The city housed us in a local hotel (out of the rain), and we were generously fed by Fred Light of the Lighthouse restaurant and service station, just up from the river.

All of this is to say that we adopted roles promiscuously for the purposes of entertainment and instruction. Playing Indian was indeed at the centre of the residence camp experience, and it had no more to do with "honouring (or even accurately portraying) Aboriginal tradition" than it did at the camps Sharon Wall studied.[53] As we did our playing, and named our junior cabins after the nations of the Iroquois, we never once stopped in, or paid any attention to, the combined Cree and Stoney reserve at the eastern end of Lake Wabamun; nor, so far as I recall, did we make anything of the fact that Wabamun was the Cree word for "mirror."[54] If we had, we would have encountered a reality very different from the ideal that Seton had propagated with the best of intentions. What's more, when our campers returned to school in the fall, the natives they read about in their school books were not the noble savages of the Council Fire, as I found when I later studied these books as an adult. Instead, they were bloodthirsty savages, pillaging and butchering and screaming in frenzy.[55] "In the world of childhood," Daniel Francis writes, "there were two Indians." One was the Indian idealized in camp, whom we admire; the other was the Indian denigrated in schoolbooks, whom we fear and pity.[56] I have no idea which had more influence on our campers. "Cultural appropriation" captures much of the first, but I think, in the end, that the man from Toronto was right: it would be simpler just to call it racist.

* * * * * *

My other major extracurricular activity was practising and performing the art of magic. When I was back at Cromdale, I became a member of the Edmonton Junior Mystic Circle, another name that brings a smile to my face as I type it out on the keyboard. We were sponsored by the Edmonton branch of the International Brotherhood of Magicians, which was the main organization of amateur and professional magicians in North America, perhaps even the world. Its annual regional conventions were very big affairs, drawing members from "rings" in western Canada and the northern U.S. Ring was the name given to local clubs, after the "Chinese Linking Rings," a classic illusion performed by many magicians, the great and not-so-great, and the magazine of the IBM was called *The Linking Ring*. I attended the convention held in Saskatoon in 1957, at the Bessborough Hotel, and one in Banff at the Banff Springs in 1959, where I won an award for "general proficiency."

Magic acts were very common in the 1950s and early 1960s, and magicians occasionally appeared on television programs like the *Ed Sullivan Show*. The Edmonton branch of the IBM—Ring #28—was pretty active, including men who performed in various genres. (There were no women in the club, except as assistants to the men, though there was a separate group called "Magigals"!) Bob Lang, for example, was an escape artist, whose appeal must have had something to do with the fact that Harry Houdini—the man who started it all—was still widely remembered, if not by people who had seen or heard of him in his own time, then in books and movies about his life. I remember seeing Tony Curtis star as Houdini in a 1953 Hollywood biopic, together with Janet Leigh—later more famous for her part in Alfred Hitchcock's *Psycho*—as Harry's wife Bess. I later acquired a vintage poster for the movie, which hung on my wall for a long time. Bob, at any rate, performed handcuff and strait jacket escapes, just like Houdini. In his act "Metamorphosis," he was tied up and secured in a canvas bag, locked into a large trunk, and then his assistant (his wife Jean) stood on top of the trunk while a kind of curtain was raised around the whole apparatus. After a dramatic countdown, the curtain fell and Bob was standing on the trunk and Jean was inside, locked in the bag. This, too, was Houdini fare. I think the popularity of magic in the fifties must have been a kind of residue of vaudeville days (as was the *Ed Sullivan Show*, for that matter), and it was not surprising that it fell off in the sixties. When Doug Henning brought it back in the 1970s, it had a post-hippie, new age flavour, and in the hands of David Copperfield it became big show business again.

There were a dozen or so members of the Junior Mystic Circle, and we would perform tricks for each other at our meetings, sometimes getting instruction from a member of the senior club. Occasionally we would assist a senior member at one of his performances, or perform ourselves as a kind of warm-up act after we had gotten proficient enough to do so. Some of the junior members were very good, both in their technique and in their stage manner. One of them, Dale Harney, who joined toward the end of my time, went on to become a professional, hosting his own television show, *Dale Harney's Magic Palace*, in Calgary.

I gradually got to the point myself where I could perform alone, and over the years I did many shows for children at Christmastime or birthdays, either in a home or in a hall rented for the occasion by a group like the Y's Men, the Y's Menettes, the West End Rotary Club, the Masons, or a cub and scout pack. Local companies—Muttart Lumber, International Harvester, Marshall Wells—put on parties for their employees and their families where I also performed. Usually I was paid a small fee, rising over time from the princely sum of $2 to $25, but I did free shows as well, at churches and hospitals, and once at a local Indian Residential School. When I was at the University of Alberta, I had friends who were members of Delta Upsilon fraternity, with the result that I performed for three years running at the annual Christmas party for children put on jointly by the DUs and the Kappa

Alpha Theta sorority. Two of the performances I remember best were in variety shows put on by the Jubilaires, a music and drama club at the university, at Convocation Hall. The first, in 1963, was called "From Bach to Bossa Nova" and the second, the following year, "Revue '64." Much of the pleasure of these came from sophisticated lighting and technical support—the shows were directed by Phillip Silver, who later became a prominent theatre designer—with piano background by Dean Charles, an early innovator in electronic piano technology. The show also attracted a large audience, at least in the second year. One consequence was that I acquired the nickname of "Mysto" in certain circles, usually uttered in the same mildly sarcastic tone that Woody had used for my outstanding teen title.

All this meant that I took my magic quite seriously. At some point I got myself a performance outfit—a Cameron plaid sports jacket that had belonged to my father, a matching tie, and a vest I had specially made. This must have been quite a dazzling sight. I purchased tables for my act that were made by Micky Hades (a stage name), who had been a member of Ring #28 before moving to Calgary and opening a magic business. Micky sold magic tricks, apparatus, equipment, and vintage posters, as well as performing professionally. The tables had felted black tops, 15 inches by 12 inches, with a short pink fringe, and they each sat on a stand that pictured a smiling, toothy rabbit emerging from a top hat. They were very nicely made and a pleasure to the eye. I still have them, though they have been packed away in a box for many years.

I also built up a small library of books on magic that I still own. Like the tables in a box, they have not been opened in a long time, except perhaps when packing for some move. They include Camille Gauthier's *Magic Without Apparatus*, Lewis Ganson's *Routined Manipulation* (all three volumes), and Geoffrey Buckingham's *It's Easier than You Think*, all of them classics of the literature on sleight of hand and close-up magic. This was my chief interest, even though I was never good enough to be a really serious magician. I always included some sleight of hand when I performed, along with other tricks—"effects," as we called them—involving apparatus. My favourite was a "multiplying billiard balls" routine, in which balls were manipulated in the fingers of one's hand, held up for the audience to see, vanishing and appearing in different ways, seemingly (one hoped) by magic.

It's hard to say what effect my brief career as an amateur conjurer had on my personal development and outlook. It must have helped my confidence, though I was nervous later, anyway, throughout my academic career, before entering the classroom to "perform" as a lecturer, especially on the first day of term. It probably eased my social relations as well, since it brought me into frequent contact with people I didn't know. It seems, at any rate, that I actually spent quite a bit of my young adulthood on stage, in one way or another.

Chapter Four
Paperback Reader

I was fortunate to arrive at the University of Alberta at a creative moment in its history. Much smaller than it was later to become—there were about 8,000 students enrolled in 1961, twice that number only ten years later—it was nevertheless in a period of growth that attracted highly capable young faculty. This was the beginning of an era of expansion that transformed universities across the country, and from which I myself was to benefit. The children of the baby boom were about to come of university age and large numbers of professors were required to instruct them. The demand was met, to a large extent, by recruitment in the United States and overseas, but it also opened up opportunities for young Canadians like me. Governments decided that higher education—post-secondary education, as it came to be called—was necessary to economic growth and modernization, and they poured enormous amounts of money into building new universities and expanding old ones. The result was a radical change in university life: in who became professors, in the nature of their work, and in their social and economic status; in who became students, in the nature of *their* work, and in their relations with their professors.

The U of A History Department in the early sixties was virtually a laboratory of what was to come. The faculty included a number of people fresh from their graduate studies, or nearly so, many of whom had been recently appointed, and the range of courses offered was remarkably wide. There were historians of the United States, Germany, France, Russia, China, and Africa, at a time when university history departments in Canada and Great Britain tended to focus on British history and, in Canada, Canadian as well. The American historian in the department, Wallace Farnham, was one of only two full-time historians of the United States in the entire country when he was appointed in 1957.[57] The man who presided over much of this growth was Lewis G. Thomas, a historian of western Canada who became chair of the department in 1958.

My introductory history course was, in subject matter, pretty standard fare for the time, a survey of European history since the Renaissance, with an introductory glance backward to the Middle Ages. It was organized, however, around books on particular subjects, rather than around a survey text. We read and discussed the books at some length in tutorials, the intervening periods between the subjects they dealt with being covered by lectures surveying bigger sweeps of time. Lectures were delivered mainly by two professors, a Christian teaching brother named John Nelson Miner, known to us as Brother Bonaventure, and a newly minted American professor of Russian history, Robert H. McNeal. Towards the end of the course several lectures were given by a graduate student, Gilbert Stelter, who was later to make a name for himself as a historian of urban Canada. My tutorial leader was another graduate student whose name I have forgotten, perhaps because his tutorials were pretty forgettable.

Bonaventure and McNeal were the heart of the course. They selected a series of books designed to capture the interest of undergraduates new to history: for the early period, Amy Kelly's *Eleanor of Aquitaine and the Four Kings*, Benvenuto Cellini's autobiography, Garrett Mattingly's *Catherine of Aragon*, and Roland H. Bainton's biography of Martin Luther, *Here I Stand*; Priscilla Robertson's social history of the 1848 revolutions, Cecil Woodham-Smith's gripping account of the Crimean War, *The Reason Why*, and A. J. P. Taylor's biography of Bismarck for the later. There may have been something on the French Revolution that I've forgotten. They gave me a taste for reading and teaching books that stayed with me. Twenty years later, I borrowed the structural idea, if not the books themselves, for a course I taught at Carleton University as Marston LaFrance Fellow. Bonaventure and McNeal also gave lectures that conveyed their own interest in their discipline and took us seriously as students, freshmen though we were. It was an indication of their teaching relationship, as well as of the religiously inflected times, that McNeal, himself of Protestant background, made a point of giving the main lecture on the Reformation expressly from what he announced to us was a Roman Catholic perspective. When I later became interested in Russian history, I was disappointed to discover that he had left U of A for McMaster University in Hamilton, though I met up with him again in Toronto, the next move in his academic career before he settled at the University of Massachusetts at Amherst.

McNeal, in fact, had not been entirely enamoured of Edmonton, which he sardonically referred to as the Athens of the North. Professors often made this kind of remark in those days, and students reacted variously to it, some enlightened by a dawning awareness of the wider world, some sloughing it off as having nothing to do with them, some resenting the sense of superiority such judgements seemed to imply. I remember hearing of a professor of political science arriving in class one morning and prefacing his lecture with a denunciation of philistine Edmontonians who had failed to show up in any significant number for a concert the previous evening by a famous visiting musician. Henry Kriesel, an eminence of the U of A English Department, was vocal in criticizing the city's (small) support for drama. The fact was, of course, that Edmonton was then a raw frontier city with little sense of its history and a commercial ethic that offered scant sympathy for the arts, which were only able to flourish with the patronage of a wealthy donor—in the circumstances, usually government at one level or another. Students were unharmed, and sometimes provoked to a detached sense of themselves, by such remarks. In more recent times, this freedom to criticize is frequently stifled by a concern not to offend local sensitivities, or it's overborne by the urge to celebrate.

The obverse of professorial independence was, in any case, a complementary student separateness. If professors could be critical of students (or their communities), students responded in kind, though in their own milieu. I think this derived, at least partly, from the formality of student-faculty relations—professors did not fraternize with students, addressed them as "Mr." or "Miss," and no student would think of addressing a professor by anything other than his or her title, Doctor

This, Professor That. This did not mean that students were necessarily obsequious or dependent. It certainly implied a hierarchy and established a certain distance, but the result was that students and professors inhabited different worlds, coming together in the classroom, in the professor's office, or in strictly defined social settings. In their own world, students made their own judgements, gentle or otherwise. One of the peculiarities of the History Department in my last two years at U of A was that it had two Lewis Thomases: Lewis G., the chair and a longstanding member who hailed from the ranching country of Okotoks, in southern Alberta; and Lewis H., a man of about the same age, but a new appointee, having left his position as Provincial Archivist of Saskatchewan a few years earlier and spent the intervening time at the University of Regina. Lewis G. was Anglican, Lewis H. United Church; the first was known among many students as "Church," the second as "Chapel."

Other nicknames were less endearing. One target of our barbs was a professor who had been born and raised in Alberta but had acquired a noticeable English accent in the course of graduate study in England. We found him altogether too tweedy for our undergraduate tastes. We must also have found something off-putting in his manner, perhaps a certain snobbishness, since Lewis G. had a bit of an English accent himself but it didn't arouse the same criticism. I was amused to read, many years later, in Gerhard Ens's history of the department—or at least of the teaching of Canadian history in the department—that Lewis G. had gone to Harvard for his Ph.D., rather than Oxford, the alma mater of his mentors, George Smith and M. H. Long, because Smith had told him he was already "too British." So, at least, L. G. had reported to Ens. It was also possible that he had chosen Harvard, like many other Canadians in the 1930s, because it was less expensive to attend, both in tuition and travel costs.[58]

Our reaction was not really anti-English, in any case. The department's Tudor expert, W. J. Jones, dazzled everyone with his effortless command of his field (and perhaps also because he was a student of the leading Tudor historian of the day, G. R. Elton). Despite the separation of student and professorial cultures, or perhaps because of it, students had a pretty good idea of what was false and what was genuine. The separation also established a standard to which we might aspire. Wallace Farnham, a very fine historian, once went off on a tangent in class about the virtues of the scholarly life, inviting those who found it attractive to indicate their interest. I think he was somewhat startled when I showed up at his door a week or so later, more or less intent on signing on. He was tolerant of my naiveté, and I went away dimly aware that maybe there was something more subtle involved.

Another teaching tandem that I encountered early on was W. J. Eccles and Barbara Fraser, who together—or at least successively—taught Canadian history. It would be hard to imagine two more different teaching styles, yet from the perspective of today what they shared is just as striking. I already had a passing impression of Eccles from the UN seminar in Banff. He was on his way to becoming the leading English-language historian of New France (his widely admired *Frontenac, The Courtier Governor*, had been published in 1959), and he taught the first half of the course. Iconoclastic in a fussy sort of way, he delivered his many and various judgements with a dry wit and a slightly uplifted chin. He seemed intent on disabusing us simple-minded westerners of any prejudices we might have of the inferiority of ancien régime French Catholic society. In those days, knowledge and understanding of New France in English-speaking Canada was still influenced, to some degree, by the views of Francis Parkman, the nineteenth-century American Protestant who had devoted much of his life to writing about the conflict between the French and British in North America, producing a widely read series of books on its evolution. Eccles no doubt exaggerated the extent of Parkman's continuing influence, but none of us in introductory Canadian history had the faintest idea that this was so, our minds on the subject of New France being pretty much blank slates. Parkman served as Eccles's foil, and we learned, among other things, that there was nothing inevitable about the ultimate British triumph in the Seven Years' War; nor, indeed, was there anything self-evidently superior about the Anglo-American justice system, and certainly nothing about British colonial relations with native Americans.

The other half of this teaching pair was a brassy young woman who liked nothing more than to arouse us out of our conventional views, either about Canadian history or about women professors. She was still working on her Ph.D., and so was "Miss Fraser" to us, though the "Miss," instead of "Professor," may also have reflected her status as a woman. Her hard-edged style belied the genteel manner of address. Years later, I was told of an encounter she had with Colonel Charles Stacey in the reading room of the Public Archives of Canada one hot summer evening in the early sixties. She and a couple of other grad students were working in the very stuffy reading room—no air conditioning at the time. Miss Fraser took it upon herself to open the three large windows at either end of the room, allowing a faint breeze to waft through, carrying with it the odours from the paper mill just across the Ottawa River. When Colonel Stacey arrived, he was in full uniform. At the time, he was a member of the history department at U of T, but he had been the official historian of the Canadian army during the Second World War and had gone on to head the army's Directorate of History for a number of years. After fetching the papers he wanted, he noticed the open windows and promptly marched over to close them. A few minutes later, Miss Fraser rose from her seat and walked over to re-open them. This happened a second time, and then a third, after which an unhappy Colonel Stacey noisily harrumphed, returned his documents to their source, and stalked out of the room, casting a steely eye on the presumptuous young woman. The others in the room smiled and chuckled. Clearly, one didn't mess with Barbara Fraser.

In the classroom she moved around more than many professors did then, occasionally walking in front of the long counter on which her lectern sat, in order to extemporize on some topic. Occasionally she would hop up onto the edge of the counter, one knee crossed over the other. It said something about her personality that she would do this in a skirt. It was not a sexy gesture, but it was daring, and a bit in-your-face. Some people didn't like this, of course—seeing it as crude and unlady-like—but this may have been why she did it. She made short work of a student (me) who was so bold as to suggest that the "A plus B Theorem" of Major C. H. Douglas, which had underlain the early policies of the Social Credit party, might have had some financial merit. The fact that Social Credit still held power in Alberta made this all the more amusing for everyone, even if my own amusement was qualified by my feeling somewhat abashed.

At the same time, both Eccles and Fraser conducted the class in more or less the same way. They arrived punctually, entering the small, tiered amphitheatre from the top, strode down the wide steps, opened their notes at the lectern, and plunged right in. Neither made much use of the blackboard, though I remember Eccles once drawing a rough sketch of an arquebus, and the forked pole on which it rested when fired, when he described a battle between natives, armed with bows and arrows, and French troops. Both Eccles and Fraser entertained questions, but their presentation and student rapport were much more formal—perhaps Fraser's a little less so—than any lecturer's today, certainly those under the age of fifty. While they departed from their notes as occasion called for, it was clear that the notes themselves were very full. This was later brought home to me in reading Eccles's *The Canadian Frontier, 1534–1760* (1969), in which entire sections of chapters seemed oddly familiar to me, until I realized I had heard the first draft of them in his lectures. I would be surprised if many professors today used their lectures as means of drafting chapters—floating ideas, perhaps, but not working them out in fully formed prose.

Fraser had written an M.A. thesis at Toronto on Sir Hector Langevin, and the *Canadian Historical Review* published much of it in a long article in 1961, rather longer than was then customary for the journal, that became the standard English-language source on Langevin's career as Sir John A. Macdonald's Québec lieutenant.[59] Sadly, it remained her only published work, since she was killed in an automobile accident, driving down the Groat Road on her way to the university in early November 1964. Her death deeply affected the U of A Department of History. I attended the funeral with my friend and fellow student, Peter Ward, to whom I have already referred, and it was evident that there was more to the emotions it aroused than sorrow at a young life cut down prematurely. In fact, Fraser had been pregnant at the time of her death, and rumours swirled about the identity of the father. The department was divided over how to respond. Open to the appointment of one of the few female professors in Canadian history departments, some members, it seems, were less open to the pregnancy of an unmarried woman. She was on her way to a department meeting where her status for the coming winter term was on the agenda when she had her accident.[60]

I had more than the ordinary student's feeling at her death because by this time—I was at the beginning of my fourth year—she was supervising my honours thesis. The honours system at U of A—"honors," strictly speaking—was quite distinct. Only a small number of students did the honours degree, three or four in history in my year, compared, say, to Ontario, where the honours degree was a very large program, taking in students by the score. Most students at U of A did the general, or pass, degree—three years rather than four—which was also the case in most other parts of the country, such as British Columbia, where I taught at the beginning of my own academic career, and Nova Scotia, where I spent most of it. University administrators moving from Ontario to elsewhere were often baffled, at least initially, by this failure of "the regions" to cleave to the Upper Canadian norm.

In any case, the honours program in history at U of A not only required a thesis in one's fourth year, the equivalent of a credit course, but it also included a preparatory reading course with one's supervisor in the third year. I've not encountered a program since that provided such intensive individual instruction to an honours student. It was undoubtedly the best part of my undergraduate program, particularly the third-year reading course that I took with Fraser. It was very demanding. I read books and articles in nineteenth-century Canadian history, producing occasional essays on my reading, the purpose of which was both to deepen my knowledge of the field and to provide some background against which to define a thesis topic. She told me, in no uncertain terms, when I came up short of what was required, but she also rewarded the effort I put out in response, telling me I learned "like a house on fire," which carried me through the remainder of the year. A friend and fellow student of hers at the University of Toronto, Robert Craig Brown, was teaching at the U of A in Calgary at the time, in the informal farm system the U of T operated for field-testing its best students, and he flew north to Edmonton (on Trans-Canada Airlines, as it was then known) every Thursday to teach two courses. I met him in Fraser's office one day, unaware that our paths would later cross again at Toronto. It was he who told me the story of Miss Fraser and Colonel Stacey after my reminiscences had appeared in *Alberta History*.

At some point in the spring of 1964, Fraser gave me a copy of a handout she had prepared on paperback resources in Canadian history for her survey course. It began, "For teachers of history one of the most interesting developments of the past few years has been the multiplication of inexpensive paperback editions of important books." I came upon it again in clearing out files one day in May 2011—retirement and departure from my office at Mount Saint Vincent University looming on the horizon at the end of June. Seized by the quaintness of this happy, if understated, declaration, I immediately walked down the hall to show it to my friend and colleague in the English Department, Karen MacFarlane, whose sense of humour I knew it would appeal to. After noting that she had been two years old in 1964, Karen reached into her bag and pulled out a Sony e-reader, paperback size, only thinner. "So you see," she said, "paperbacks were just a fad." It was at this moment that I realized that my scholarly and intellectual life, as a student and professional historian—not to mention as the owner of a bookstore in the village of Elora, Ontario from 1975 to 1980—coincided with the rise, flowering, and (modest) decline in Canada of that new publishing form. I had spent the previous half-century as a paperback reader.

By the end of my reading course with Miss Fraser, I had settled on the Treaty of Washington of 1871 as my honours thesis topic, but now, of course, I needed a new supervisor. Lewis H. Thomas, who arrived in 1964, stepped in, or was commandeered, I never knew which. He left me pretty much on my own, probably because he hardly knew me, as I him. This was fine with me. The vast amounts of money the Alberta government was investing in the university—and in its branch in Calgary, soon to break off as the University of Calgary—meant that the library was able to spend freely on the acquisition of materials in microform, such as all the Canadian newspapers then being microfilmed under the aegis of the Canadian Library Association, and on the purchase of out-of-print books and primary sources, such as government documents, from antiquarian book dealers. It also maintained standing blanket orders for all new books coming out of the expanding publishing programs of scholarly presses.

A new library was built to house the growing collection, and I spent much of my time in my fourth year in the basement of the Cameron Library, reading parliamentary debates and sessional papers in print and newspapers on microfilm. When I was not in the reading room, I was upstairs in my carrel in the "stacks," which were open for the first time to ordinary students. This meant one could browse for books and collect them on one's own, without having to hand in a request slip at the circulation desk and wait for it to be delivered by a member of staff. Another of the library's features indicative of the era was that each floor had a smoking room, where students could study without giving up—or even giving pause to—their cigarette habit. I was one of them. The smoke was often thick in the confined space, which can only have blurred any distinction between first-hand and second-hand smoke.

Within a few years, many of the rising stars of the department had moved on. McNeal was gone to McMaster and Eccles to Toronto by my third year, Lewis Hertzman, the department's modern German historian, shortly after that to York University in Toronto, and Donald Wiedner, a historian of Africa south of the Sahara who wowed his classes with intricate maps drawn freehand on the blackboard as he lectured, to Temple University in Philadelphia. Brian Heeney, a British historian and son of the eminent diplomat, A. D. P. Heeney, went to Trent in Peterborough, and Wallace Farnham to Wyoming. I vaguely sensed that the break-up of this cadre of new people had something to do with Barbara Fraser's death, and the emotional upheaval that followed, but other factors undoubtedly played a part. There were many opportunities for movement by the mid- and late sixties, and two of the departures occurred before her accident. Both York and Trent were brand-new universities, for example, founded to meet Ontario's exploding demand for new student spaces, and professorial mobility was greater than it had ever been before, or has been since. The department had to build itself anew.

Faculty I knew from other departments left as well. Eli Mandel, from English, who was making a name for himself as a poet, went to York. He had been one of the faculty who had participated in a seminar series offered to high school students that I had attended in Grade 12, reading from Lawrence Ferlinghetti's recently published collection of poetry, *A Coney Island of the Mind* (1958). Robin Mathews, another poet, who was also a nationalist and prominent critic of the Social Credit government, went to England before eventually returning to Canada. George Melnikov, with whom I had studied Russian, and Bohdan Bociurkiw, who gave a course in Russian politics and government that I had taken in the political science department, both went to Carleton. Money alone was not enough to keep ambitious faculty in the Athens of the North if they wished to go elsewhere.

* * * * * *

Nothing better illustrated the transitional character of the time than the History Club. It had been founded by A. L. Burt, for a long time the leading English-language authority on the "Old Province of Quebec"—Quebec after the Conquest—a year after he arrived to take up a teaching post at U of A in 1913. Burt's model had been the Historical Club at the University of Toronto and in my day it operated much as it had for the previous half-century. It met in a faculty member's home of a Saturday evening, hosted by the professor whose turn it was, and equally by his wife, who laid on a spread for our somewhat nervous consumption after the evening's business was done. A few professors attended, as well as students—who had nothing better to do on a Saturday night!—and guests were invited from the community. The guest of honour on one occasion was Morden H. Long, a retired professor emeritus who had been head of the department in the late forties and early fifties, and who had published his first book in Canadian history, on early explorers of the Northwest, in 1919. Then well into his seventies—that is, about my age now—he seemed unbelievably ancient to us.

The professors' wives who presided over refreshments were also distinguished by the fact that they were the only females present, unless one of the three female faculty members of the department happened to attend. Amazing as it now seems, the History Club was closed to women, and I have to say that I hardly noticed at the time. The exclusion was one way among many, according to Donald Wright in his history of the professionalization of history in Canada, that male historians engaged in "boundary work," the demarcation of who belonged in the trade and who did not. Clubs such as ours were part of the selection process, initiating potential candidates into the *arcana* of professorial behaviour. Those who attended received invitations, though I don't remember mine. No big thing was made of the exclusion, at any rate, until Sylvia Van Kirk complained a year or two after I graduated, eventually becoming president. She later told Wright—by this time she had become an eminent historian herself of the fur trade, and particularly of the role of native women in the trade—that someone had said that the Club would turn into a "hen party"under a woman president.[61] I should add that there was also a club on campus exclusively for women of a literary and intellectual disposition, the Blue Stocking Club, which had been founded by A. L. Burt's wife, Dorothy.

History Club meetings were formal affairs, one of the few semi-social occasions on which students and profs got together. We all wore jackets and ties and were on our best behaviour, especially since a professor's home was socially a cut above the settings in which most of us usually found ourselves. In my memory they were all rather dark—maybe it was just the Edmonton winters—and the atmosphere sombre as we sat around a living room listening to a fellow student deliver a paper. The formal dress was actually not the feature that most distinguished the event, since most of us often wore ties and sweaters or blazers to class, while girls were usually well-turned out in skirts or dresses. Jeans on men or slacks on women were rarely seen on campus in the early sixties, apart from the small group of "beats" who hung around the Tuck Shop. A girlfriend I once brought to a family gathering created quite a stir, much to her own amusement and slightly to my discomfiture, by showing up in a long, loose-fitting sweater, black tights, and dark glasses.

Child of the Fifties

One's nervousness at the History Club was less a matter of concern for how one looked than for how one conducted oneself in the presence of one's teachers—and also, of course, for how successful one's paper would be. Presentation of a paper was the central event of the evening. Usually it was something someone had written for a seminar, perhaps further honed and polished. Since no one attended all seminars, and not all seminars were organized around the presentation of papers, the material was new to most of the audience, whether students or faculty. When my turn came, at the 277th meeting of the Club, one Saturday night in late November 1964 (not long after Barbara Fraser's death) at the home of L. H. Thomas, I gave a paper on the Dreyfus Affair that I had written for Frederick De Luna's seminar in modern French history. It made no particular mark.

The case had been far different, at least as far as I was concerned, when Brian Dippie had given a paper to the Club on his favourite subject, George Armstrong Custer. This was the first time that I thought that one of us—that anyone I knew as one of my peers—might actually be a real historian. Brian probably knew as much about Custer and the Battle of Little Big Horn as anyone, even as a student, much less later on, when he wrote his first book about it. He had been immersed in the subject for years as a hobby. His paper was on the Custer myth and how it variously represented Custer as hero or villain, depending on current political and ideological needs. His command of his material was a marvel in itself, but he turned it to new and startling effect in an extended epilogue on how similarly John F. Kennedy, whose assassination had occurred only a few months before, was already undergoing mythification, and how views of Kennedy might also serve in future as a barometer of changing values and interests. It was a *tour de force*. Brian went on to do an M.A. at Wyoming (attracted, in part, by Farnham) and a Ph.D. in American Studies at the University of Texas.

The Kennedy assassination was the first occasion, in my memory, on which it was said that everyone remembered exactly where they had been when they heard the news, so shocking and significant it was, and so immediately was it transmitted around the world. Like so many others, I can still visualize the circumstances. I was in a classroom at noon, sitting about halfway back in the row by the windows, waiting for Professor Heeney to arrive to deliver a lecture in British history. He entered through a door almost exactly opposite my desk, strode to the front of the room in a state of concentrated energy, frown on his face—in contrast to his usual sunny smile—and announced in mid-stride that President Kennedy had been shot. One of the students (Dieter Buse, I think) exclaimed, "Oh, my God," and the room fell silent, followed quickly by a rising general murmur. Heeney cut it short by launching into his outline for that day's lecture, which he characteristically wrote on the blackboard, something few professors did in those days. (Truth to tell, some of us thought this was pretty Mickey Mouse, having no idea that it was the way of the future, much less that a few decades hence most professors would be providing a running outline in PowerPoint that would continue for the entire class.)

Another such event that occurred more recently was the felling of the towers of the World Trade Center in New York City on September 11, 2001, thereafter inscribed in our minds (and diminished) by the shorthand "9/11." This time, too, I was at a university, only now as a professor myself, and I found the roles reversed. I happened to wander into the little room allocated to the student History Society at Mount Saint Vincent, where I found a student from one of my classes, Greg MacLean, listening intently to a portable radio. This was around ten o'clock in the morning and just what was happening in New York had not yet become clearly apparent. A plane had crashed into one of the towers, possibly by accident, but then a second plane had flown into the other tower. The possibility that this had been purposeful was so alien to the newscaster's mind, and those of his listeners, that its meaning was difficult to assimilate. Not long afterwards, the towers crumbled.

Heeney's business-as-usual attitude fifty years earlier may have been tactical, an attempt to maintain calm. If so, it was certainly successful. I rather think, however, that it was a mark of the terrible event having happened elsewhere, and therefore not calling forth a radical break from routine. After class we all went off for lunch as usual at the cafeteria—"Hot Caf," as it was called—though conversation was everywhere about Dallas and the shooting of the president. A friend made a rather tasteless remark, verging on schadenfreude, about Jacqueline Kennedy, another indication of the foreign-ness of the event. Nevertheless, one marvels, looking back, at the thrall in which we were held by the aura of the assassination. It was partly the shock of the new—the assassinations of Martin Luther King and Kennedy's brother Robert lay in the future—and partly the effect of concentrated media attention. Television had come to Edmonton less than a decade earlier, and coverage of the events of the following days was almost continuous, while footage of the assassination itself and the subsequent swearing in of Vice-President Lyndon Johnson, Jacqueline Kennedy at his side, was replayed time and again. Two days later, I was watching at home when Lee Harvey Oswald was murdered by Jack Ruby, live on television (so to speak), in the midst of a crowd of reporters, police, and officials. Shock aside, it was almost as if the border had been momentarily obliterated and all this were happening in my own country instead of a foreign nation, albeit one with which we had close ties.

For the previous decade or more, those ties had seemed rather too close for comfort to many Canadians, giving rise to a gradually building wave of nationalism, including (as at times in the more distant past) a strong component of anti-Americanism. The Massey Royal Commission on National Development in the Arts, the Gordon Commission on Canada's Economic Prospects, the pipeline debate that had brought down the Liberal government in 1957, and the nationalist posture adopted, if somewhat erratically, by the Conservative government of John Diefenbaker had all reflected and encouraged the new nationalism. So also had the publishing company McClelland and Stewart's initiation of the New Canadian Library and the Carleton Library series, leading examples of the paperback publishing explosion Barbara Fraser described in her handout. In the more immediate background of the assassination were the Bay of Pigs invasion in 1961, the Cuban Missile Crisis in 1962, and the climax, in the 1963 election, of the dispute over whether Canada would agree to accept nuclear warheads for the Bomarc anti-aircraft missiles it had acquired five years earlier. Again a government fell, this time Diefenbaker's, and the new Liberal government of Lester Pearson immediately accepted the warheads, an action that was to produce the landmark nationalist text of the sixties, George Grant's *Lament for a Nation*.[62]

I was not self-consciously nationalistic at the time, as I was later to become, but I did have a sense of national identity. I had no doubt that I was a Canadian citizen, even if (as I also knew) I was at the same time a British subject. Looking back, I have also come to realize that an unspoken assumption of my sense of identity was that my Scottish heritage somehow made me more Canadian than non-British immigrants, who were "foreigners." Those who had come to Canada in the course of the twentieth century from Italy, China, Japan, Ukraine—or even earlier, from Germany, for example—were commonly referred to by their ethnic origin as well as their Canadian citizenship. The idea of the "hyphenated Canadian" was expressly rejected by John Diefenbaker, but it was common to speak of Ukrainian-Canadians, Chinese-Canadians, and so on—or even of "Ukrainians" or "Chinese." I don't remember anyone referring to my parents as Scots-Canadian, even though they were immigrants. I think this was the result of Canada being a part of the British Commonwealth. British immigrants—at least those who were white—didn't assimilate so much as simply move from one part of the Commonwealth to another. The term "English-Canadian" was less a mark of immigrant origin than a linguistic and cultural designation of one of the two "founding peoples" of the country, the other of course being "French-Canadian." No one at the time acknowledged Indigenous peoples as founders of Canada. Ethnic hyphenation was a mild—sometimes not so mild—form of discrimination.

My idea of Canada was also *national*, not local or provincial, and while I had no knowledge of Ottawa, I had an idea of national government. I was receptive to Diefenbaker's nationalism, and that of his Saskatchewan lieutenant, Alvin Hamilton, which was an anti-localist, anti-provincialist sort of nationalism—*One Canada*, as Diefenbaker entitled his memoirs.[63] Perhaps for this reason, or simply because the news was dominated by the growing enmity between Diefenbaker and Pearson, and (in 1964) by the debate over a new flag, I have no memory of the three most important pieces of legislation passed by the Pearson government, which mark it as one of the most significant of the twentieth century: the Canada Pension Plan, the Canada Assistance Act, and Medicare. I joined with a group of other like-minded students, led (I think) by David Shugarman, who later became a political scientist at York University, in forming a new campus party, the Constitutional Party, the chief plank of which was to uphold and expand the powers of the federal government.

Part of the identity I felt in the sixties was the awareness of Canadian difference from the United States that underlay my reaction to the Kennedy assassination. I had a sense of Canada as a "middle power," a member of the "Western alliance" but at the same time a kind of fellow traveller of those countries that pursued neutrality in the Cold War and those, sometimes the same, that had recently achieved national independence or were in the process of doing so. The international order of which I was aware, if only superficially, included the Colombo Plan, Jawaharlal Nehru, Kwame Nkrumah, the Suez crisis and the UN Emergency Force, and Dag Hammarskjold among its chief points of orientation. This awareness must have had something to do with my attendance at the UN seminar in Banff, though CBC News was also responsible, particularly its foreign correspondents and, among them, especially James M. Minifie, whose book, *Peacemaker or Powder-monkey: Canada's Role in a Revolutionary World* (1960), made a strong case for Canadian non-alignment.

The CBC also made me aware of cultural differences. I noticed at the time that representations of the Canadian past on CBC television were very different from their American counterparts. Admittedly, my knowledge of the latter was limited pretty well to TV westerns, but CBC historical dramas and documentaries were not nearly as lively or colourful, and they seemed reluctant to romanticize or mythify—"Radisson" (1957), for example, vs. "Davy Crockett" (1954–55). In fact, they had something of the excitement of Earl Cameron reading the nightly news. This sober sensibility may have been the result simply of financial constraints, rather than of the CBC's public service ethos, or perhaps it was an expression of its relatively highbrow culture, or its tradition of documentary realism.[64] I may also have been especially receptive, since the teacher in high school who had kindled my interest in history, Harold Anderson, had done so by giving me an appreciation of dull facts, drily presented. Whatever the reason, I took from the CBC and Mr. Anderson a suspicion of heroes, and the glimmer of an understanding that the past was different as history than it was as myth. In later years, when it had become a cliché to say of Canadian history that it was dull and in need of enlivening, I used to say to my students that, yes, Canadian history *was* dull but that was what made it interesting.

Despite my dawning awareness of Canadian-American differences, I managed to carry on my historical studies, for the most part, with little sense that they had much to do with my own personal life. I was certainly a serious and conscientious student, interested in national and world affairs, but my interest in history—notably Russian, British, and Canadian—was academic and intellectual. I didn't choose my courses or essay topics because my personal or family background led me to them, or because I had already developed an amateur interest, like Dippie. In fact, I regarded this detachment as a personal shortcoming, and only gradually grew into my discipline as a vehicle for understanding my place in the world. It was perhaps partly for this reason that I later found J. H. Hexter persuasive (as I've already noted) in arguing against the relativistic proposition that historians inevitably approached the past through the prism of their own experience and beliefs, and that, in fact, it worked the other way around just as often. One's study of the past shaped one's response to the issues and events of the present.

In any event, in studying the Treaty of Washington, in which British negotiators were more concerned with sustaining the Anglo-American relationship than with defending Canadian interests in the fisheries or demanding compensation for the Fenian Raids, and American negotiators were single-minded in defense of their own interests, I felt my own patriotic feeling rise, for all the effort I expended on a careful, objective analysis of treaty negotiations. My patriotism, as I later realized, was a rather limited anglocentric pan-Canadianism. I was only dimly aware of Québec and even less so of the Maritimes and Newfoundland beyond. Nova Scotia may have penetrated my consciousness for the first time in a personal way when I heard of other history students at U of A taking jobs with the Fortress Louisbourg restoration project. When I later read W. L. Morton's *The Canadian Identity* (1961), however, Frank Underhill's *The Image of Confederation* (1964), George Grant's *Lament for a Nation* (1965), Ramsay Cook's *Canada and the French-Canadian Question* (1966), Pierre Elliott Trudeau's *Federalism and the French Canadians* (1968; *Le Fédéralisme et la société canadienne-française*, 1967), Marcel Rioux's *Quebec in Question* (1970; *La Question du Québec*, 1969), and Margaret Atwood's *Survival: A Thematic Guide to Canadian Literature* (1972), I had been well primed. These were the referential texts of "the sixties," and it is difficult to imagine them having the impact they had in English-speaking Canada were it not for all the nation-making thought and action of "the fifties" before them. When I wrote a paper on anti-Americanism in the first decade of the twentieth century for Craig Brown's graduate course in North American history at Toronto, my motivation was political as well as historical.

✷ ✷ ✷ ✷ ✷ ✷

Small numbers in senior-level seminars made for a closely knit group of students at U of A. We were also required to sit field exams in the final year of the honours program, another unusual undergraduate requirement, which we did alongside the M.A. students. The prospect of writing exams on an all-or-nothing basis was daunting to us all, drawing us together in shared trepidation. Besides Dippie, my history group—not all of them in the honours program—included Stan Gooch, who went on to a career in External (later Foreign, now Global) Affairs in a time when this was deemed a natural career choice for history graduates; Terry Eastwood, who later pioneered archival studies at the University of British Columbia; and two older Scotsmen, Frank McKenna and Charles Cowan, both quite recent immigrants. Frank and Charlie seemed to get through their undergraduate history degrees with relative ease, on the strength of their Scottish public schooling. Both of them thought for themselves and deferred to no one simply because of position. "Bullshit baffles brains" was one of their more pungent aphorisms, serving them both as an ironic rule of life. Charlie's home and family formed a warm social centre, and when he was later appointed to the History Department at the University of Victoria, he urged both Brian and me to apply for positions there, then played no small role in persuading his new colleagues of our merits. We both arrived in Victoria in the fall of 1970. I'm pretty sure it was Charlie, a year behind me and Brian in the honours program, who had said the History Club would turn into a "hen party" if a woman became president.

When I began my undergraduate degree, I had no idea that I would end up going on to graduate school or become a professor of history. A combination of deepening interest, success, the example of my peers, and the encouragement of my teachers led me to apply for admission to graduate studies at Columbia University, Carleton, and the University of Toronto. I can't remember why I applied to Columbia, where I was turned down in any case. Offered places at Carleton and Toronto, I chose Toronto. There I discovered friends and fellow students from all over the country. Some of them were better prepared than I was for graduate study, but Alberta had given me a pretty good foundation and a sense of possibility.

In the half-century since, universities have changed dramatically, for better and for worse. In becoming larger they have become more impersonal but at the same time far more inclusive. The student body at Alberta had grown significantly since World War II and comprised many students (including me and many of my friends) who were the first in their families to attend university, but it was still predominantly middle class, WASP, and male. One result of the formality of classes and student-faculty relations was that students who required extra help or encouragement seldom got it, and those who fell beyond the "boundary work" of belonging had to work that much harder to win acceptance. The breaking down of barriers has been unquestionably for the better, as has the removal of inhibitions about putting outlines on the board or on PowerPoint, or whatever it is that professors use today. Discussion now takes place even during lectures, provided the lecture is not taking place in a hockey arena, and professors actually make their assignments and expectations clear at the beginning of a course.

On the negative side of the ledger, the language of economic growth that persuaded governments to invest in university education when I was a student is now just as persuasive in justifying reductions of funding in the interests of efficiency and rationalization. The investment then was so great that it was possible for the arts and humanities to participate in expansion almost unnoticed, whereas today, in circumstances of restraint, their defenders find it necessary to justify them as studies that *really do* have practical utility, just as much as other studies that contribute more directly to innovation, productivity, labour force development, and so on. Universities have taken on much of this language themselves, in mission statements and strategic plans whose primary purpose is to demonstrate accountability to the governments that supply a diminishing proportion of their revenues, and in treating their students as customers or clients whose success can be measured by various indices of customer satisfaction. Professors, meanwhile, often claim to have clean hands in the corporatization of universities, while concentrating on their own form of productivity, pursuing the gospel of research that was only beginning to dominate the job of a professor in the early 1960s. Students often take second place.

Left: Ken in Elorabooks, late 1970s

Right: Dewar-Copp home on the upper Alma side road

Below: Terry, Reuey, Linda, Monica, Marged, Megan, Helen in front of house

Left: Ken, Marged, Megan, and Helen in new half of duplex

Chapter Five
The Sixties

"The sixties," in myth and history, does not refer to the years from 1960 to 1969, nor even necessarily to a ten-year period. What it means varies from person to person and place to place. For Mark Phillips, a friend who immigrated to Canada from the U.S. as a draft resister in the summer of 1968, and whom I met shortly afterward, the sixties were indeed more or less the decade of the 1960s. He had already immigrated once before, to the U.S. from South Africa with his family in 1957, a background that primed him for various acts of resistance as a teenager, beginning with participation in the anti-nuclear senatorial campaign of Harvard historian H. Stuart Hughes in 1962, followed by joining in the March on Washington for Jobs and Freedom the following year, when Martin Luther King delivered his "I Have a Dream" speech. Resistance to the Vietnam War was not something new for Mark, but an escalation of tensions that had been building for some time in the U.S.

Some of the variety of "the sixties" may be seen at Mount Saint Vincent University, where I spent most of my career. Until 1966, the Mount was a Roman Catholic university for women, the only independent institution of its kind in the country, and the professor standing in front of most classrooms would likely have been a member of a female religious order, teaching in a tradition that stretched back (broadly speaking) to Marie de l'Incarnation, even if the order that founded the Mount, the Sisters of Charity of St. Vincent de Paul, was American in origin. There were a few male clerics and lay persons, female and male, on faculty. Some years after I arrived in 1982, I learned from Pierre Payer, a philosopher and former priest, that when he had entered his classroom for the first time after coming to the Mount in 1968, he was startled to see all the students rise from their seats. When he recovered his equanimity, he told them they could sit down. He later found out that they had been expecting him to begin class with a prayer. In one of my early classes, I had a student who was returning to the university to upgrade the degree she had received in 1971. She told me there had then been strict rules prohibiting the wearing of slacks by women and the admission of male visitors (the university had become co-ed in 1967) to the all-female residence. At the same time, however, the sister appointed president of the Mount in 1965, Catherine Wallace, was quite familiar with second-wave feminism and set about reforming—or revolutionizing, in the view of one recent scholar—certain aspects of the university on feminist lines, including the introduction of one of the first women's studies courses in the country, which later led to the development of a pioneering women's studies program.[65]

My own experience was different again. My sixties began in 1965 or 1966, which also means that my "fifties" extended into the early sixties. In fact, in contrast with those who argue for a "long sixties," from the mid- or late 1950s to the early or even mid-1970s, I'm inclined to think in terms of a "long fifties," like Julian Barnes.[66] My sixties coincided with my initiation into graduate studies, and lasted until the early seventies. This was still a couple of years after 1963, the date offered by Doug Owram, a later historian of the period, as the (approximate) beginning of "the sixties" in Canada.[67] In Owram's telling, there were two overlapping "sixties": one was that of the hippies and counterculture, the other that of political activism. Mine was very definitely the activist sixties, even if my hair was long and my trousers were bell bottoms. I think this may have had something to do with the fact that I was not, strictly speaking, part of the baby boom generation, with whom the sixties are often identified, but was born in 1944, two years before the start of the "boom," though it is also true that the seriousness of mind and purpose that marked my own sixties, and that I associate with Hilda Neatby in the fifties, was a feature of sixties figures as well, many of my friends among them.[68] In my experience, the foundation of much of the change that undoubtedly occurred in the sixties had been laid in the long fifties.

Child of the Fifties

* * * * * *

I set off for Toronto in the late summer of 1965 in a Volkswagen 1500 that my mother had purchased a year or two before. She did not drive herself and I had served as chauffeur, as well as having the car for my own use—taking my turn in the car pool to university, for example. She generously gave it to me so that I could drive across the country and use it in Toronto. I have a photo of my fresh-faced, short-haired self on the morning of my departure, standing beside the car, the photo having been taken by Uncle James, who was visiting from Scotland. The car was a blue coupe with its engine in the rear, though it also had a luggage compartment above the engine, in addition to the one in front. The 1500 was a very fine little car, comfortable and "peppy," as my father used to call responsive cars. It marked the beginning of Volkswagen's efforts to expand its line in North America beyond the Beetle that had made its reputation for compact car efficiency.

I had never before driven such a long distance, much less across the prairies and lakes to Ontario's towers (to adapt Oscar Brand's then-popular folk anthem, "Something to Sing About"). It was a very long drive, though I've forgotten how many days it took, and it gave me an impressive sense of the vastness of Canada, a sense that did not diminish no matter how often I made the trip in later years as I moved from Toronto to Victoria with my wife Marged, back to Toronto and southern Ontario, on to Ottawa and "up to the Maritimes," by then with our two children, Megan and Helen. In 1965, when I finally arrived in Toronto, I drove down Avenue Road from Highway 401 to the point where it passes between the provincial legislature on one side and Hart House on the university campus on the other, buildings in both cases (I noted) that were historic rather than modern. Reaching College Street, I turned right and pulled into a parking spot in front of the Lassonde Mining Building. I got out, put some money in the meter, and was looking around to get my bearings when Garry Clarke, a friend from Edmonton who was doing graduate work in geophysics at U of T, bounded out of the building's front door and down the steps onto the sidewalk. He had seen me out the window of his lab in one of the upper stories. This was a fortuitous beginning.

I had applied unsuccessfully for a junior fellowship at Massey College, the graduate residence that had opened two years before in conscious imitation of the colleges of Oxford and Cambridge. Garry was a junior fellow and I think it was he who had suggested I apply, despite the widely held perception (of which he was well aware) of Massey as a reflection of the upper-class pretensions of its patron, former Governor-General Vincent Massey. The appointment of the novelist Robertson Davies as its founding Master had only strengthened the perception, as I learned in my first years in Toronto. With Massey ruled out, I had applied for a room in the Sir Daniel Wilson residence of University College, an undergraduate men's residence that accepted a few grad students, and had been accepted. That's where I was generally headed when I ran into Garry.

Sir Dan, as it was known, had its own English college flavour, as I soon discovered. It was divided into six "houses"—mine was McCaul House—offering single rooms to residents, a common room for relaxation, and a large dining hall where everyone took their meals. One's first contact was with the Hall Porter, who kept track of who entered, at least in theory, and provided various services, notably distribution of the mail that residents received. Each house was presided over by a don, who was responsible for keeping order and enforcing rules, such as the hours allowed for female visitors, and for encouraging an atmosphere of community. While breakfasts and lunches were provided, cafeteria-style, over a certain period of time, dinner hours were fixed and formal. Everyone wore a gown and stood by his chair until "High Table"—the dons and other officials, sometimes the dean of UC—arrived and a perfunctory grace was said (*Benedictus benedicat*). Not so different from the Mount, in its way, though I doubt the women behaved quite as raucously as the men. Few, in fact, took the dining hall ritual and ceremony very seriously, but it was intended to convey an old-world sense of decorum in university life. Much of the formality, including gowns, came to an end within a few years.

I settled in pretty quickly, soon discovering that one of the few students who had his breakfast as early as I did was an intellectually inclined freshman from McCaul named David Cluff. Over the ensuing year, David and I became good friends. Another friend I made early on was Gerry Friesen, a grad student in Canadian history from Prince Albert, Saskatchewan, whom I met in the long line that formed for registration at the School of Graduate Studies, which was located in an older building just south of the residence on St. George Street. Gerry was sharing a house near the university with other students and invited me to join them, thinking I would prefer accommodations that were independent of the university. I was quite happy where I was, however, perhaps because it was my first time living away from home for an extended period, perhaps because of a general timidity. In any case, I had already made a financial commitment to UC. This proved to be a good decision, since I became a don myself the following year, which meant, among other things, that I paid almost nothing for my room and board for two years of grad school, in return for exercising a moderate level of supervision over residents.

The M.A. program at Toronto had recently been modified, with a view to expediting a student's progress on to the Ph.D.. Instead of requiring a thesis, which tended to drag on, sometimes for several years, it was now possible to do a "course work" M.A. as an alternative, in which students completed three full-year courses in history—this was before semester-long courses became the norm—plus a "cognate essay" (or "2000 paper") in one of the courses. The 2000 paper was a kind of mini-thesis, longer than a regular essay and based largely on primary research, but intended to be sharply focused and limited in scale. Students were allowed a maximum of one calendar year to complete the program, but almost everyone I knew finished at the end of the academic year. In effect, the M.A. year and the year following constituted two years of course work prior to study for comprehensive exams and embarking on research for one's doctoral dissertation. An indication that the M.A. retained some major significance, at least for me, is that my mother and sister flew down from Edmonton to attend my convocation in May.

I wrote my cognate essay in a course on the history of Canada from 1860 to 1921 taught by Donald Creighton, who was the senior Canadian historian in the department and widely considered to be pre-eminent in his field.[69] He was certainly one reason why many students chose to do advanced study at Toronto. At a time when few history departments in English-speaking Canada had developed graduate programs with national reputations, Toronto was the default choice for many, at least for those who wanted to work in Canadian history, but the individual members were also part of the attraction, Creighton in particular. His first book, *The Commercial Empire of the St. Lawrence, 1760–1850* (1937), had been especially influential—presenting, according to one later historian, what "may be the only genuinely arresting paradigm ever to emerge from Canadian historical scholarship"[70]—but his biography of John A. Macdonald, published in two volumes in the 1950s, had a similar impact, not least because of its evocative prose. Some of us may have questioned this assessment—J. M. S. Careless's "metropolitan thesis" was also insightful in its approach to Canadian history, and his biography of George Brown was the equal of Creighton's Macdonald—but there was no doubt of Creighton's greater stature in the historical community. He was also shortly to have a perceptible political impact on many of us.

The subject of my essay, the establishment of the Canadian high commissionership to Great Britain in 1880, seems quaintly old-fashioned today—as, for that matter, does the Treaty of Washington that I had studied for my honours essay. I was taken back to the atmosphere of my student years in late November 2016 when I read a "Lives Lived" column in the Toronto *Globe and Mail* by the historian Duncan McDowall, remembering his former colleague in the Carleton University history department, David M. L. Farr. McDowall remarked ironically of Farr's Oxford doctoral dissertation on the British Colonial Office that it was "hardly the stuff of trendy, modern historiography."[71] One can hardly dispute the judgement, and since the book Farr produced on the basis of his thesis was a major source for both my honours and cognate essays, it unmistakably suggests that they both might similarly be described. It was only a few years later that historical writing in

Canada took the socio-economic (and, for many, Marxian) turn that displaced political, diplomatic, and constitutional history for the next few decades.

Farr's work, McDowall suggested, had been in tune with the "then-transcendent theme" of Canadian historical writing, the country's gradual evolution from "colony to nation," a phrase that had achieved especial renown in the title of a general survey written by the Queen's University historian A. R. M. Lower and published just after the Second World War, *Colony to Nation: A History of Canada* (1946). This was the undoubted theme—and over-arching argument—of Creighton's course, though its point was very different from Lower's. The topics taken up in our weekly seminar included Confederation, the National Policy, Dominion-Provincial Relations (as they were then known), the Manitoba Schools Question, the Alaska Boundary Dispute, and the like. Students were assigned one of two or three sub-topics for research and presentation—one of mine was "Sir John Macdonald's status at the Washington Conference of 1871." Creighton listened intently to all of these, sitting at his desk at the head of the long table at which we all sat—all seminars were held in professors' offices, Creighton's being rather larger than most—and looking contemplatively out the window, his hands joined together in an inverted "V" under his chin. Most of us were slightly awestruck in his presence, referring to his middle initial "G." as standing for "God," rather than "Grant," his middle name. Often topics focused on a particular historical document, and he would direct penetrating questions to the presenter as part of the discussion. The atmosphere was far from casual, but it was also respectful and not without occasional humorous moments. What the presenter did not want was for Creighton to rise from his chair and launch into his own analysis of the topic or document in question, pacing back and forth from bookcase to window, which implied that the presentation needed some serious straightening out.

The high commissionership was a benchmark on the road to nationhood, marking the achievement of a measure of control over the country's external relations. While Creighton approved of my treatment of the topic ("an excellent survey," he wrote, giving it a grade of

A–), he commented that I might have been more adventurous in my conclusion, linking the new office to the growth of cooperation with Britain in defence and foreign affairs over the long term, in which the mother country granted the colonies a voice in policy in return for their assumption of greater responsibility. He was not closed to alternative arguments and explanations, but it was clear in his comments here, and in the course as the whole, that in his view the evolution to nationhood had occurred in association with Britain, rather than in opposition to it, and that it had been led by Macdonald, Charles Tupper, and Robert Borden more than by Alexander Mackenzie and Wilfrid Laurier (much less William Lyon Mackenzie King, whose prime ministership lay beyond the boundaries of our course). "Or in other words," he went on, posing a decidedly rhetorical question, "is Borden, rather than Laurier or King, Macdonald's logical successor?" The imperial connection had been a benefit to Canada, not a cost, and it had not precluded the development of an autonomous Canadian nationality, with a Britannic touch, one element of which was suspicion of the United States. This was not at all Lower's take on the story of nationhood, which conceived of Canada as North American in character, more than Britannic, and of the British Empire as an obstacle, rather than an aid, to national development. This was also the view of the even more liberally inclined Frank Underhill, who had been Creighton's colleague for many years, until he had departed for Ottawa in 1955. Tensions between them figured largely in the department lore of which newcomers like me gradually became aware.

If Creighton and Lower differed sharply in their interpretations of evolving nationhood, they shared the view that it constituted the primary theme in the history of Canada. They also shared a similar understanding of the role of the historian, which was to serve as custodian of the nation's past; in Lower's words, introducing *Colony to Nation*, he hoped his book would "help Canadians to some of that self-knowledge so necessary if they are to take their rightful place in the world, and still more, if they are to be a happy people, at peace with themselves." Today, this seems hardly less quaint as an aspiration than the subject of my cognate essay. "Certainly on no-one," Lower continued, "is the duty of revealing to the people reasons for the faith that is in them more directly laid than on the historian, for by its history a people lives."[72] This passage featured prominently in the presidential address I heard delivered at the first meeting of the Canadian Historical Association I ever attended, in 1967 in Ottawa. The national message may have been prompted, in part, by the fact that it was Centennial Year, but it was not at all inconsistent with the general approach of the man giving it, Richard Saunders, with whom I had just finished a course in historiography that was required for the Ph.D. program. The topics we took up in our weekly seminars all contained a moral that Saunders sought to draw out in discussion. It was not surprising that his own view was the same as Lower's, as he revealed early in his address: "Whether the historian wants it or not he is cast in the role of guide and mentor to the nation."[73]

One result of the priority they gave to the historian's role in nation-making is that historians had a wide audience; not a mass audience, by any means, but one that included a broad reading public. An index of the breadth can be found in the Governor General's Literary Awards for non-fiction, which in the twenty years after the war included Lower among the recipients (for *Colony to Nation* and again for *This Most Famous Stream: The Liberal Democratic Way of Life*), Creighton (twice, for each volume of his Macdonald biography), Careless (for his general history, *Canada: A Story of Challenge* and for his Brown biography), W. L Morton (for his history of the Progressive Party), and Underhill (for his collection of essays, *In Search of Canadian Liberalism*). Academic historians have not disappeared from the award lists in the years since, but they have become rare birds, despite the much larger number of books they now write. One recent exception is Bill Waiser of the University of Saskatchewan, who won in 2016 for his history of Saskatchewan before it entered Confederation as a province in 1905. Another indication of the earlier breadth of readership is the remark made by the journalist Robert Fulford in 1966, that historians were "the great social thinkers of Canada, the people who shape our souls and define our aims." Among the examples he cited were Creighton, Underhill, William Kilbourn, and Ramsay Cook, whose collection of essays, *Canada and the French Canadian Question*, he was reviewing at the time.[74]

Creighton had made only occasional political interventions in the past, unlike Underhill, who had been politically engaged continuously for forty years, but in the sixties he plunged into the major national debates of the decade, over Canada's relations with the United States and, domestically, over Quebec's place in the federation and the status of the French language. He assumed the role, not so much of an intellectual criticizing public policy, as of a reluctant Jeremiah unleashing waves of invective against those who had betrayed the country's destiny as he saw it.[75] He joined with other conservatives in condemning the direction in which successive Liberal governments had led the country. Most notable among them was George Grant, whose *Lament for a Nation* was published in 1965, specifically in response to the Liberal government's decision to accept nuclear warheads for the Bomarc anti-aircraft missiles that had been acquired by the previous government, led by John Diefenbaker's Conservatives. More generally, Grant condemned the triumph of continentalism in Canada and the dominance of American liberal capitalism. Another conservative who entered the fray was W.L. Morton, who had delivered a series of lectures that were published as *The Canadian Identity* in 1961.

In 1969, a few years after I finished my M.A., Creighton delivered an address to the CHA annual meeting entitled "The Decline and Fall of the Empire of the St. Lawrence." This was a remarkable event, which I described in an essay I wrote jointly with Mark Phillips, criticizing the "professionalization of history," the tendency of modern historians (as we thought) to write for a narrow audience of fellow historians, rather than a broader public, and for their own professional advancement, rather than the public interest.[76] The auditorium—it may have been a gymnasium—was packed with hundreds who had come to listen to the country's most prominent historian, yet I thought Creighton seemed "quite out of place, not only in the thesis he was arguing, Canada from colony to nation to colony, but in his whole style." The audience was attentive, but largely unsympathetic, and at the end no one took up his invitation to challenge and question. I wrote that Creighton seemed like a "relic from the past" in a hall full of younger professionals, and his address "his valedictory performance."

Creighton's posture and the substance of what he wrote were both a part of his appeal for those of us who had come to regard the Vietnam War and American ownership of the Canadian economy as evidence of U.S. imperial overreach. One result was an odd alliance of conservatives and socialists on a number of issues in the late sixties, which (together with the creative mind of the political scientist Gad Horowitz) generated the proposition that, historically, there had been an affinity between conservatism and socialism in Canada, based on a tory collectivism that stretched back through the government activism of Sir John A. Macdonald in building the Canadian Pacific Railway to the United Empire Loyalists, who had fled the incipient liberal individualism of the American Revolution to settle in the northern colonies and elsewhere.[77] Horowitz drew on the work of the American political scientist Louis Hartz, whose seminal book, *The Founding of New Societies*, argued that the settler colonies of Europe were "fragments" of their originating European societies and were fundamentally shaped by the ideologies dominant at the moment of their founding, or "point of departure."[78] The U.S., he argued, was a liberal fragment, which explained the failure of socialism to take hold in American political culture. Horowitz argued that socialism had found a place in Canadian political culture because the origins of English Canada in the Loyalist exodus (and early nineteenth-century British immigration) meant that it had a "tory touch." Tory collectivism, unlike liberal individualism, made it possible for a socialist collectivism also to develop in tension with it. In addition, French Canada was a feudal fragment in its origins, which made a liberal consensus of the American variety impossible. Approaches to history were very much influenced by politics in the sixties.

It was in this context that Creighton found an audience among young activists on the left. Relic from the past he may have been, but that was part of his attraction. The same might be said of George Grant, whose *Lament* was later described by his nephew, Michael Ignatieff, as "a masterpiece of grief and anger."[79]

★ ★ ★ ★ ★ ★

My interests, as I realized much later, lay more in intellectual history than social history, even at this early stage. The evidence lay partly in the essays I wrote for my other graduate courses. In Russian history, for example, which I studied with my old first-year instructor, Robert H. McNeal, my term paper was on the ideas of Nikolai Chernyshevsky, one of the leading revolutionary populists of the nineteenth century, and particularly on his view of relations between Russia and "the West," one of the touchstone issues of debate among the Russian "intelligentsia." Rejecting the nationalism of the slavophiles, who claimed for Russia a unique messianic role in world history, Chernyshevsky nevertheless also rejected the constitutionalism of western liberals and called for revolutionary change based on the organization of the peasant commune. No Marxist himself, he was regarded by later Soviet historians as a precursor of Marxism-Leninism, pointing to, among other things, Lenin's borrowing of the title of Chernyshevsky's 1863 novel *What is to be Done?* for a political pamphlet of his own. My essay was based on Chernyshevsky's journalistic and other writings, some of them in Russian, which McNeal noted in his comments. At some point during the year I asked him whether he thought specialization in Russian history might be a good idea, since I had enrolled in his course half-thinking that it might become my major field. He took my inquiry seriously, but recommended in the end that I stay with Canadian history, where the prospects of a job were much better. The result was that nineteenth-century Russia became one of my two minor fields.

My other minor was nineteenth-century Britain, where I took a course from Richard Helmstadter, a mildly eccentric young historian of religion in the Victorian era. It extended my horizons in more ways than one, since among the books on the required reading list was E. P. Thompson's recently published *The Making of the English Working Class* (1964), which was shortly to become the bible of the new social history, shifting the focus of working class studies from institutions and organizations to the experiences of working men and women and their growing consciousness of class; which is to say, shifting the focus from labour unions to the working class. My paper for the course was on the little known satirist Thomas Love Peacock, whose novels were witty and sharply observed commentaries on issues of the day, "the day" being mainly the early part of the century. My primary sources in this case were the novels, including some that were unpublished during his lifetime, and some of Peacock's published correspondence. Helmstadter encouraged me to revise the paper and submit it somewhere for publication, which I did, sending it off to *Victorian Studies*, the leading journal in the field. This may have been a tad too ambitious on my part. In any event, they turned it down and I didn't do anything more with it.

My interests were even more evident in my choice of Canadian literature as the "outside minor" required in the Ph.D. program. Gordon Roper, a member of the Trinity College English Department, offered the course. He was one of the pioneers in the teaching of "Can Lit," having begun by slipping a couple of Canadian titles onto the end of his undergraduate course in American literature, which he had introduced a few years after the Second World War, when department courses were all English in nationality as well as language.[80] By my time, he taught Canadian literature courses at both the undergraduate and graduate levels. The course opened up a new world to me—the novels of Thomas Chandler Haliburton, Sara Jeanette Duncan, Morley Callaghan, Frederick Philip Grove, Sinclair Ross, Margaret Laurence, Robertson Davies, and others. Many of them I purchased, and still own, in their New Canadian Library editions (Miss Fraser's paperback explosion again), all of them priced under two dollars. It is a remarkable fact of Canadian life for my generation that we did not grow into a knowledge of our literature, as did our contemporaries in the U.S. or our descendants today, but rather came to it abruptly and purposefully, as we learned that there had actually been Canadians before us who had written of the world on the basis of their local experience.

Roper was hardly unique, as I later discovered. Much of the impetus for Can Lit courses came from a landmark conference at Queen's in 1955 on the theme of "The Writer, His Media and the Public." Co-chaired by F. R. Scott and Roy Daniells, it was attended by established writers like Callaghan and Dorothy Livesay, and younger ones like Eli Mandel (who offered the first course in Can Lit at Alberta in 1962–63), Adele Wiseman, and Leonard Cohen. The conference gave rise not only to new courses, but to other ventures, including the New Canadian Library series and the journal *Canadian Literature*.[81] It was only one way in which the national feeling of the sixties was rooted in the fifties.

Roper's course was quite heavily enrolled, for what was ostensibly a seminar, but it was interesting and enjoyable nevertheless, partly because of his ease in the classroom and his infectious enthusiasm for the books we read. I was not the lone historian enrolled amongst the English students—Gerry Friesen was another—and others also helped to enliven discussion, inside and outside of class, notably Joan Murray, who later went on to become an art historian and director of the Robert McLaughlin Gallery in Oshawa. I wrote my term paper on Grove, whose novels I found absorbing and intriguing, especially in light of a study of American literature by Leo Marx, *The Machine in the Garden: Technology and the Pastoral Ideal in America* (1964), which led me to organize my paper around the theme of Marx's sub-title. I later submitted a revised version to the *Journal of Canadian Studies*, which had been established at Trent University in 1964 as an interdisciplinary journal focused on Canada, part of a wider initiative at Trent, under the leadership of its first president, T. H. B. Symons, to promote Canadian Studies. The paper became my first scholarly publication.[82]

I'm not sure exactly when I had first been drawn to fiction. My childhood and adolescent reading had been pretty narrow—besides the books I mentioned earlier that I read in Scotland, I remember Hardy Boys mysteries and, occasionally, nineteenth-century romantic novels whose popularity had persisted (*Treasure Island*, *The Three Musketeers*, *Swiss Family Robinson*). By university, however, my horizons had broadened enough that I found myself so absorbed by Dostoevsky's *Crime and Punishment* that I continued reading it far into the night even in the midst of my fourth-year final exams at U of A. At Toronto, I somehow found myself in a circle of friends who were doing English degrees, notably Don Rubin, who had graduated from Oberlin

College and come north for grad study. Don was shy and opinionated at the same time, and interested especially in English Catholic novels, and even more especially in the novels of English converts to Catholicism—Graham Greene, Evelyn Waugh, Muriel Spark. Garry Clarke was also a friend and the three of us often got together, sometimes for a meal at the Maison Suisse on Bloor Street, a restaurant presided over by a worldly European woman who was always seated in a booth near the front and who acted as the *maitre d'*. Restaurants were very much a part of Toronto's modern sophistication, as a result primarily of postwar immigration. One night, the three of us spent an evening talking in Rubin's apartment on Spadina Road north of Bloor, at the end of which we decided to head over to Palmer's, a lunch counter next to the Park Plaza Hotel, at Bloor and Avenue Road. I had my car—why, I'm not sure—and we drove south on Spadina to the Bloor Street intersection. As I was about to turn left—on the green light—a car drove through the red light on Bloor and broadsided us. I vaguely remember returning from hospital in the early morning hours, all of us luckily only shaken up by the accident. That was the end, however, of my VW 1500.

Friendship with Rubin, and with a few others, was as much an education as any of the courses I took. I was soon deep into English novels, not only those of Greene, Waugh, and Spark, but also C.P. Snow, Christopher Isherwood, Ford Madox Ford (the subject of Rubin's M.A. thesis), and Anthony Powell, whose novel cycle, "A Dance to the Music of Time," led me into Marcel Proust's "Remembrance of Things Past" and, much later, Hugh Hood's "The New Age" series. Over time, I developed the habit of reading in binges—all of someone for a period of time, someone else for another period, which had the benefit of giving one a sense of an author's body of work, as well as immersing one in another world. A few years later, I spent a summer reading Balzac, Flaubert, and Stendhal. It worked for lighter reading as well—the mysteries of Dorothy Sayers, Marjorie Allingham, Ngaio Marsh, Cyril Hare, Edmund Crispin, and Michael Innes; the spy novels of Eric Ambler, John Buchan, Erskine Childers, and John Le Carré. Not all of this was prompted by Rubin, but he was a stimulating companion.

I gradually realized that he was gay, though the term was only coming into general use at the time and gays were still pretty much in the closet. This was just about to change, or begin to change. In 1967, Pierre Trudeau, as federal minister of justice, introduced legislation decriminalizing "homosexual acts" performed in private—"There's no place for the state in the bedrooms of the nation," he famously said, quoting a *Globe and Mail* columnist, Martin O'Malley. Here was a change that did not have roots in the fifties, it's safe to say, when I had visited Mary Imrie and Jean Wallbridge with my mother in their house in the suburban woods. Still, it was some time before it became common for gays to "come out." Others I knew married and only later publicly acknowledged their sexual orientation. This must have created considerable personal tension and may have been partly responsible for Don's highly strung personality. He spent the better part of a year travelling in Europe in 1969–70, and after settling in London for several months his letters perceptibly shifted from neurotic to contented. Later, Marged and I visited him in Montreal, where he taught at McGill University, and again in Vancouver, when he had left academia entirely. We then lost touch and it was only recently, when I read a volume of poetry by his best friend in Toronto, Betsy Greene, that I discovered that he had died in the HIV/AIDS epidemic of the 1980s. Betsy remembers him in one poem, "my almost brother," "eyes full of light that saw / right into the core of people and books." He carried the spirit of the sixties, she writes, "trying to speak true."[83] This was also the Rubin I knew.

Another friend was Don Kubesh, whom I met in Creighton's seminar and got to know when some of us would go out for a beer of an evening. Donald was his own person. He had graduated from the University of Manitoba, spent a year playing professional football for the Saskatchewan Roughriders, and returned to Manitoba for an M.A. He was a no-nonsense kind of guy and good in an argument—well-suited, in fact, for the profession in which he ended up, which was law. He used to pride himself in travelling light, claiming that he could move all his worldly possessions, if necessary, in his VW Beetle. We experimented with marijuana in his third-floor flat in Rosedale and on a few other occasions. I never became a user myself and was later embarrassed to expose my amateur roll-your-own skills one evening in Victoria at a friend's apartment, and again with another friend in Halifax. I just never caught the habit, even though I was a cigarette smoker, and neither did Donald. He also steered pretty clear of the educational radicalism that I took up in the late sixties. The issue that captured his interest was aboriginal rights, and he became deeply sympathetic with the native reaction to the 1969 federal White Paper on Indian policy that was expressed by Harold Cardinal in *The Unjust Society: The Tragedy of Canada's Indians* (1969). I too was sympathetic, but never as emotionally involved. We went to see Arthur Penn's movie of *Little Big Man* when it came out in 1970. Donald was so revolted by the cavalry attack based on the battle of the Washita that he got up and left.

He had a personal impact on my future, at least indirectly, when he linked up with a woman from Edmonton, Nancy Wildgoose. I knew Nancy slightly from U of A, as I also knew Marged Thomas. When Marged came to Toronto for library school in 1967, she shared a flat on Kendal Avenue with Nancy and another woman. Sometime in the fall of that year, the four of us went out together on a double date, though I'm not sure we called it that. Marged and I discovered we had much in common, including a love of books and movies—or films, as we called them then. Ingmar Bergman, Frederico Fellini, Jean-Luc Goddard, Francois Truffaut, Claude Chabrol, Luis Buñuel, and others were revolutionizing the making (and viewing) of films in the 1960s. "Hollywood" became something of a dirty word, except for the odd American director who was influenced by the Europeans, like Penn. Film societies and repertory theatres competed with the commercial movie houses. We often went to film showings in rooms with portable projectors and screens, presided over by nerdy enthusiasts—one in particular I remember, in a red sweater with a shawl collar, introducing the night's selection at length, arms waving. He was almost as entertaining, in his way, as the film. In any event, Marged and I soon became an item, eventually sharing an apartment together.

Morning coffee in the Hart House cafeteria was another occasion for meeting and getting to know people. More often that not, this happened mid-morning when a number of us left our carrels in the stacks of the Sigmund Samuel Library and walked the short distance over to Hart House. Barrie Dyster, an Australian student, was a late riser and usually began his day at about this time, always showing up with a copy of the Manchester *Guardian* sticking out of his shirt pocket, a sign of his seriousness as well as his Britannic orientation and his politics. Barrie lived in a flat in Yorkville, near the Riverboat coffeehouse, where rising folk singers like Joni Mitchell often appeared. It had a kind of outdoor deck at the back, over the lower floors, and was the site of several enjoyable parties. Barrie was a delightful companion.

Another person I learned a lot from was Ian Lumsden, a graduate student in the department of political economy. We met in the fall of 1966, when we both took up positions as dons in Sir Dan, he in Taylor House, me in Hutton. Ian was Anglo-Argentinian in origin and he was doing his doctoral research on Fidel Castro and the Cuban revolution. His supervisor was the eminent neo-Marxist political theorist C. B. Macpherson, whose magnum opus, *The Political Theory of Possessive Individualism: Hobbes to Locke* (1962), was required reading for anyone on the political left at the time, as were his Massey Lectures, *The Real World of Democracy* (1965). My political education—or consciousness-raising—came from various sources, but one of them was definitely Ian. On weekday evenings after dinner, most of us who had eaten at High Table, including guests, adjourned to the Senior Common Room for coffee or tea. When discussions became especially lively, it was often because Ian had taken a radical position on some issue of the day, frequently moving one of the other dons, another political scientist, to outrage. This other don, whose name I don't recall, was a liberal, a term Ian almost always used with mild contempt. It was a commonly held belief in the late sixties, at least on the left, that liberalism had exhausted itself in the course of the twentieth century, reaching its nadir in justification of American imperialism.

It was against this intellectual backdrop that I followed the rise of Pierre Elliott Trudeau in the Liberal party and his pursuit of the party leadership in the late winter and spring of 1968. I remember watching the leadership convention on television with several other people in Ian's apartment in Sir Dan. (The previous week we had also watched

Lyndon Johnson announce his withdrawal from the American presidential race: "I shall not seek, and I will not accept, the nomination of my party for another term as your President." We cheered.) Conventions were exciting affairs in those days, when delegates met in an arena—the Ottawa Civic Centre in this case—to listen to speeches, cheer on their favourites, and then engage in guesswork and horse trading in a succession of votes winnowing the candidates down to a final victor. It took four ballots, starting at 1 p.m. and finishing just before eight in the evening. After the first three ballots, defeated candidates and their supporters showed up in the sections of the remaining contenders, shaking hands and picking up signs to wave from the stands. In the end, Robert Winters, the Anglo candidate of big business, was runner-up. The Liberal press was enraptured by Trudeau's style and relative youth. On the following Monday, the *Toronto Star's* front page carried a huge colour photo of him taking in the results and looking both overjoyed and slightly bemused. The lead story opened with a reference to his age, forty-six, while inside, on the op-ed page, the paper's Ottawa editor, Peter C. Newman, described him as representative of a "new generation."[84]

I decided to try my hand at writing an essay on Trudeau's victory, arguing that it presented the illusion of change in the Liberal party while masking the reality of continuity, and backing it up with references to Liberal leaders in the past and especially their views of Canadian-American relations and the French-Canadian question. Ian mentioned my piece to his friend Cy Gonick, the editor of *Canadian Dimension*, who invited me to send it in for his consideration. The essay promptly appeared in the next issue, leading a section of three pieces on Trudeau, the other two written by Gad Horowitz and Walter Young, a political scientist at the University of British Columbia.[85] This was highly gratifying and I had Ian to thank for it. In the next issue, a letter appeared from Ramsay Cook, who had left the NDP to join the Liberals in support of Trudeau, chiding me for writing in my conclusion that Louis Stephen St. Laurent had been regarded in Quebec as more Stephen than Louis, and now Trudeau was similarly more Elliott than Pierre. This gave me pause—was this vaguely racist of me?—but

I had talked this over with another friend, Ken Wyman, and decided it was a legitimate comment on his federalism and hostility to Quebec nationalism.

After two years as dons, Ian and I moved out at about this time and rented an apartment on Kendal Avenue, up the street from Marged and Nancy, and north of Sibelius Park, a charming green oasis one square block in size. This was a perfect urban location at the time, in the "Annex" neighbourhood west of Spadina, before most of the properties had been priced out of the reach of anyone but the very well off. The apartment was a large two-bedroom, stretching from front to back of an older three-storey building. We were on the third floor. That autumn, Ian—always full of energy—became the organizer of the latest project of the University League for Social Reform, an organization of Toronto academics whose name and purpose recalled the League for Social Reconstruction of the 1930s, regarded by many as the "brains trust" of the CCF. ULSR ("ulcer") was progressive in its orientation, but included people of a wide range of views. Carl Berger, for example, who was pretty conservative, and Craig Brown, who had become my thesis supervisor, had contributed to an earlier volume, *Nationalism in Canada*.[86] Ian's subject was the Americanization of Canada, and participants were more decidedly leftist, though they also included Michael Bliss, a young liberal historian (and fellow grad student) who was shortly to make his name as a historian of Canadian business. I helped with the organizing, acting as secretary at meetings, most of which, in any case, were devoted to the presentation of papers. I botched one aspect of a secretary's job, later losing the records I had kept. The book that resulted drew a fair bit of attention, a sign of the nationalist times.[87]

Another mark of Ian's energy was his involvement in various activities related to Cuba and Latin America. On one occasion, after a conference on Latin America somewhere in Toronto, he came back to the apartment with a number of conference-goers, including Ivan Illich, who had been a featured speaker. A charismatic radical priest, Illich had founded the Intercultural Documentation Centre in Cuernavaca, Mexico several years before, whose purpose was to offer language courses, but mainly to re-educate priests, missionaries, and community organizers from elsewhere, and especially the United States, about how to conduct themselves in "underdeveloped" countries, particularly by learning about the indigenous people's culture before learning their languages. Catherine Wallace served at Cuernavaca in the summer of 1964, before becoming president of Mount Saint Vincent University.[88] Illich came at issues from an oblique angle, perhaps because of his complex background (Jewish and Catholic, Austrian and Croatian) and ecclesiastical experience, though he left the institutional church around this time.[89] His international reputation was to grow in subsequent years with the publication of a succession of short polemical books, including *Deschooling Society* (1971), *Medical Nemesis* (1976) and *Gender* (1982). United by a common critique of institutional modernity, his books forced one to think outside of conventional ideological categories. They became part of my own cultural awareness.

Another person I came to know who was involved in Latin American interests was John Foster, a grad student in Canadian history who also had Craig Brown as his thesis supervisor. John was an early member of the Latin American Working Group, which started in 1966 with the aim of educating the public about Latin America and promoting Canadian government policy that was independent of the United States.[90] This meant, among other things, steering clear of the Alliance for Progress and the Organization of American States, creatures fostering U.S. interests. John was from Saskatchewan and came out of the Student Christian Movement and the peace movement, expressed in the Student Union for Peace Action (SUPA) and, before that, the Combined Universities Campaign for Nuclear Disarmament (CUCND). He was one of the few people I knew who lived his political beliefs, sharing a house communally with a number of other people. This was not all sweetness and light, by any means, but it is an indication of John's commitment to principle that he did his best to work through the issues that arose, including after he got married and had a child. His relations with Brown were rocky, much worse than mine, which were less than ideal, but it is another indication of his commitment that he eventually finished his thesis on Canadian Protestant missions in China. He went on to spend most of his adult life serving in various international humanitarian causes, including a number of years as national secretary of OXFAM Canada.

Latin America attracted general interest at the time, partly because of a book by Andre Gunder Frank on the relation of capitalism and underdevelopment on the continent, especially in Chile and Brazil. It became the basis of dependency theory, which had wide application. Frank drew on a variety of disciplines—economics, history, anthropology, sociology—to criticize the conventional liberal view that underdevelopment was the condition of a traditional society before it modernized, or (in its Marxist form) of a feudal or neo-feudal society before it made the transition to capitalism. On the contrary, Frank argued, underdevelopment was a process of capitalism itself, deriving from one of the basic structures of the capitalist system, the interaction of metropolis and satellite, or centre and periphery. The surpluses produced in colonial societies under capitalism were expropriated, in whole or in part, by the metropolis through the agency of privately held corporations, which in modern times had assumed monopoly form. The concept of surplus came from two of the men to whom Frank dedicated his book: Paul Baran, a leading American Marxist economist who died prematurely in 1964, and Paul Sweezy, another Marxist, who founded the magazine *Monthly Review* in New York and the publishing house Monthly Review Press, which published Frank's *Capitalism and Underdevelopment in Latin America*.[91] I purchased their books in the late 1960s, in some cases having seen reviews of them in *Canadian Dimension*, which I tore out and inserted inside the front covers, where they remain today. They and a number of others made up a reading list of books that would never have made it onto the lists of the courses in which I was formally enrolled—books by the Cambridge Marxist economist Maurice Dobb; by Harry Magdoff, a co-editor at *Monthly Review*; by the critical theorists Herbert Marcuse and Erich Fromm, both prominent members of the Frankfurt School; by the neo-Marxist sociologist Barrington Moore Jr.; and by the German emigré scholar George Lichtheim, among others.[92] They made up a kind of counter-course of books that many people I knew were reading and discussing. Canadian content was notably absent, with a few exceptions, such as John Porter's *Vertical Mosaic*, which attracted a wide audience immediately on publication in 1965, though Porter was no Marxist.[93] Baran and Sweezy's *Monopoly Capital*—referred to in discussion simply as "Baran and Sweezy"—later helped to shape my thinking about the role of the state in economic development, along with Ralph Miliband's *The State in Capitalist Society* (1969).

* * * * * *

My political reorientation did not occur overnight. Shortly after I arrived in Toronto, in October 1965, I attended the "Toronto International Teach-in" at Varsity Arena, joining some 5000 others in listening to a series of speakers addressing a variety of issues, including the war in Vietnam. The idea for the teach-in—the term was a play on "sit-in," the non-violent form of protest used in the American civil rights movement—had originated in a conference held earlier in the year at the University of Michigan, where the first teach-in had been held in March in reaction to the U.S. bombing of North Vietnam. The purpose of the conference had been to discuss ways of building on the success of the March event and others that had followed elsewhere in the U.S. One person who attended was Charles Hanly, a philosopher at U of T, who put forward the idea of an international teach-in in Toronto.[94] I knew nothing of its origins and my memory of the teach-in itself, as of so much else, is vague, apart from the feeling—sitting high up in the stands at Varsity Arena—of taking part in Something Big, though I do remember the presence of Staughton Lynd, the American historian and vocal opponent of the Vietnam War, Fenner Brockway, the British socialist and pacifist, and George Grant, who all spoke at one session.

"It was a phenomenon, this teach-in," as Myrna Kostash was later to write in an early history of the decade.[95] The organizers were remarkably ambitious. They sought speakers from far and wide—not only the U.S., Britain, and Canada, but France, the Soviet Union, Guyana, Cambodia, China, South Vietnam, and the National Liberation Front in North Vietnam. Their hope was to stimulate exchange between different points of view around the central theme of revolution, and even to contribute to peace efforts by bringing together people who otherwise would never have met. Their hopes did not pan out. China refused to send anyone to an event that described itself as neutral in relation to the imperialist U.S. and the unreliable USSR, and after a number of complications no one came from the NLF in the end. The anticipated presence of the NLF led to difficulties getting a representative of the U.S. government, and the Americans who did come were academics. Even at that, one of them threatened to withdraw if a grad student from Berkeley who proposed to represent the views of Hanoi was allowed to participate. The grad student was excluded, to the annoyance of many students who attended. The Russian who spoke was from *Pravda*.[96]

All of these efforts followed from Hanly's premise that the purpose of the teach-in was educational. Others on the organizing committee, such as Mel Watkins and Abe Rotstein, whom I was later to meet through ULSR, disagreed, thinking it was primarily a vehicle of protest, like a sit-in.[97] For my own part, innocent that I was, the teach-in seemed capable of being both. Reading Hanly's introduction to the collected speeches today, I am reminded of Brian McKillop's contention that Canadian thought in the mid-twentieth century was marked by a continuation of the moral imperative that had animated so much thinking a hundred years before, despite the secularization that had occurred in the interim. While moral concern was hardly unique to Canada, it had informed critical inquiry over several generations, constituting a distinctive tradition of Canadian thought. McKillop cited the novelist Hugh Hood, who wrote in the early 1970s that "a real integrity of conscience" lay at the core of the Canadian experience, in which "compromise and squareness, far from being dirty words, are recognized as what they are, the vital and necessary complement of commitment."[98] Apart from the implicit claim that there actually *is* a tradition of Canadian thought, which is arresting in itself, this is an insight that I once thought helped to explain the writings of Hilda Neatby and the culture in which I grew up in the 1950s, and suggests a continuity from the one decade to the next.

Hanly's high moral seriousness is evident in his earnest announcement at the beginning of his introduction that the only thing we could be certain of in a world fraught by a sense of uncertainty and impotence was that, "the more understanding we have of the conflicts that are making the great historical events of our age, the better."[99] He tells his readers that neither the book nor the teach-in itself offered any definitive answers to the questions of the day; instead, they brought together representatives of the contending points of view so that the conflicting "philosophies and policies" could be drawn out. One part of their purpose was to get beyond the almost-automatic anti-communism of western governments and opinion makers; another was to show that resolution of conflict could not be left to chance but had to be expressly pursued through conciliation. Nowhere in his essay, or in the book as a whole, is there a hint of the playfulness that marked the emerging counterculture of the time, nor of the irony and relativism characteristic of the present day.

Moral concern was even more apparent in the speeches of Lynd, Brockway, and Grant, whose session was entitled "Revolution and the Citizen's Moral Responsibility." Both Lynd and Lord Brockway posed the dilemma of how to *act* on one's moral principles, Lynd in the circumstances of a democrat in a democratic country in which a majority of people seemed to support the war, Brockway recalling how he had felt compelled to give up his absolute pacifism during the Spanish Civil War of the 1930s, when he had firmly supported one side over the other in a violent conflict.[100] Grant, who at the time was the head of the religion department at McMaster University, began his address with a forthright statement that his position was that of "a Canadian nationalist and a conservative." Departing from Lynd and Brockway's challenge to aspire to the perspective of humanity at large, he declared that one's moral responsibility was grounded in the kind of system in which one found oneself. In Canada's case, we were becoming a satellite of the American empire, which severely restricted our room to maneuvre. He shared the New Left's abhorrence for the "emptiness and dehumanization" of modern technological society, but he thought it was deluded in its hopes for change: hope for the future was "the chief opiate of modern life," he said. One's moral obligation was to face reality and to "use our intelligence and our love to open up areas where human excellence can exist."[101] There was nothing easy about any Grant message, as I was to learn.

Not every speaker at the teach-in was a moralist. Cheddi Jagan, for example, the former president of British Guiana (as it then was), was a Marxist who argued that the problems of Latin America were structural and rooted in the domination of the American "business industrial complex," and other speakers had similar points of view on problems elsewhere in the world.[102]

Yet the unmistakably moral purpose of the teach-in was an indication that the Marxism that was to strongly influence responses to American imperialism later in the decade had yet to take hold, except in a few radical quarters such as SUPA. I suspect that if it had been organized a few years later its guiding principles would have been very different. It may have been this moralism that drew me in and led me to re-examine my own world view (such as it was). Moving leftward politically, in these circumstances, was less a matter of conversion than of a growing awareness of different points of view, and perhaps a coming of age, in the midst of others doing the same.

Chapter Six
Innocent Abroad

I have a box full of old clippings, magazines, and assorted documents, the remains of a collection that I now regret culling some years ago. One of the items I did not discard was the May 1967 issue of *The Realist*, a wildly satirical magazine published in newsprint form by Paul Krassner, a one-time writer for *Mad* magazine. This was the issue that carried a poster-like centrefold by Wally Wood, an illustrator for *Mad* and other comics: the "Disneyland Memorial Orgy," depicting numerous Disney characters engaged in various indecent acts. Snow White is in the left centre, for example, surrounded by the Seven Dwarfs, one peering down her blouse, another with his hand up her skirt, and so on. The issue also contained an article that achieved even greater notoriety, "The Parts That Were Left Out of the Kennedy Book," which purported to be passages cut from William Manchester's *The Death of a President* at the behest of Jacqueline Kennedy. The book had just been published, and it was widely reported that Mrs. Kennedy had demanded that a number of passages be removed from the manuscript. The invented excisions concluded with an account of Jackie returning to Washington with her husband's body on Air Force One after his assassination, and coming upon Lyndon Johnson crouching over the corpse, sexually penetrating the bullet hole in Kennedy's throat.[103] Krassner was one of many in the sixties who erased the boundary between what was acceptable and what was shocking in public discourse. He was also a member of Ken Kesey's "Merry Pranksters," who crossed the U.S. eastward from California in 1964 in a psychedelically painted bus, dropping much LSD along the way. The trip became the subject of Tom Wolfe's *The Electric Kool-Aid Acid Test* (1968), a pioneering venture in the New Journalism.

Another item in the box, perhaps of greater lasting value, is a landmark essay by Noam Chomsky that had appeared in the *New York Review of Books* a couple of months earlier, in February. The *New York Review* had been started in 1963 with the aim of improving the quality of book reviewing in the U.S. and had quickly established itself as a premier journal of political commentary as well as literary criticism. Chomsky's essay, "The Responsibility of Intellectuals," confirmed (and radicalized) the journal's reputation and established his own as a leading American intellectual.[104] A *tour de force* of barely contained moral outrage, the essay attacked the hypocrisy and dishonesty of liberal intellectuals—such as Arthur Schlesinger, Jr., and Walt Rostow in the Kennedy and Johnson administrations—who served as apologists for American policy in Vietnam. "It is the responsibility of intellectuals," Chomsky declared, "to speak the truth and to expose lies," which he proceeded to show wasn't as simple as it sounded. Writers like Irving Kristol, editor of *The Public Interest* (and emerging father of neoconservatism), only fudged the issues when he distinguished between "responsible criticism" and the "teach-in movement," with its "unreasonable, ideological types." Others, like former National Security Advisor McGeorge Bundy, lied outright when he claimed that, "American democracy has no taste for imperialism." Reading the essay today, its power is somewhat diminished by its extravagant assertions, but it made for riveting reading at the time. Chomsky would not have been out of place at the Toronto International Teach-in.

I mention these two items partly because their presence in my archive is a reminder that the line between political activism and the counterculture was by no means fixed. Reading matter aside, the same sort of cross-over existed in music. The vibrant American protest song tradition was carried forward into the 1960s by folk singers like Pete Seeger, Bob Dylan, and Joan Baez, and even by Peter, Paul and Mary, though they were decidedly more mainstream. Dylan famously blurred the line between folk and rock when he went electric in 1965, eliciting boos from some members of the audience at the Newport Folk Festival. Rock music itself became a form of protest as it moved away from the rock 'n' roll of Bill Haley and Buddy Holly, and morphed into the psychedelic rock and folk rock of the Jefferson Airplane with its lead singer Grace Slick, Big Brother and the Holding Company with Janis Joplin, the Doors, the Band, and the Byrds. In addition to the civil rights movement, racial conflict, and the Vietnam War, one's attention in 1967 was also taken by the Monterey Pop Festival and the "Summer of Love" in Haight-Ashbury, San Francisco, not to mention the Beatles and their release of "Sergeant Pepper's Lonely Hearts Club Band" early that summer, which took everyone's breath away. Locally, Seiji Ozawa became something of a counterculture figure in the world of classical music when he served as conductor of the Toronto Symphony during these years. With his Beatles-like mop of hair, he was a magnetic force on the podium.

Apart from the odd Canadian singer, like Leonard Cohen and Joni Mitchell (and adoptee Jesse Winchester a little later), and the "British invasion" (the Rolling Stones as well as the Beatles), the popular music we listened to was overwhelmingly American, which brings me to my main reason for mentioning *The Realist* and Chomsky's essay. They were both published at a time of rising nationalism in Canada, which was shortly to find expression in centennial celebrations and the love-in that was Expo 67 in Montreal. One component of that nationalism, at least in English-speaking Canada, was anti-Americanism, as it had been for much of the country's history, waxing and waning as circumstances allowed or required. Its origins lay partly in the United Empire Loyalists' rejection of the American Revolution and the migration of many of them northward in the 1770s and 1780s. For a long time its political and ideological associations were with Conservative politics and thought, the other side of the coin of attachment to the British Empire. John A. Macdonald used it to great effect in the election of 1891, when he argued that Liberal support for "unrestricted reciprocity" with the U.S.—free trade, more or less—would lead to annexation, and Robert Borden used it again twenty years later in the reciprocity election of 1911, with similar success. My term paper for Craig Brown's seminar looked at anti-Americanism in the Conservative party in the decade up to and including the 1911 election and concluded that it was politically effective when the threat of American domination seemed real and could be linked to the opposing party; otherwise, it had little impact or remained dormant. The Liberals, for their part, tended to be more open to the U.S. and, as time went on, more critical of Britain.

This conventional alignment was upended in the 1960s. John Diefenbaker, it's true, had rocky relations with the Kennedy administration, and Lester Pearson seemed to be acting in the traditional Liberal mode when his government accepted nuclear warheads for the Bomarc missiles, which so provoked George Grant. Nevertheless, Pearson also appointed Walter Gordon as his finance minister in 1963. Gordon had already sent up warning signals about foreign investment in the Royal Commission on Canada's Economic Prospects that he headed in the late fifties, and his first budget proposed a tax on foreign takeovers of Canadian corporations, arousing such opposition that it had to be withdrawn. After resigning from the government in 1965, he returned two years later and appointed the Task Force on Foreign Ownership and the Structure of Canadian Investment, chaired by Mel Watkins, which became a major stimulus of economic nationalism. Gordon went on to join with Mel Hurtig, Abraham Rotstein, Peter C. Newman, and others to form the Committee for an Independent Canada in 1970 to promote economic nationalism. For an old-fashioned small-l liberal like Frank Underhill, who had moved from the CCF-NDP to the Liberal camp after the progressively-minded Pearson had been chosen leader, it was all rather baffling. Invited to write the foreword to the University League for Social Reform's collection of essays on nationalism in Canada, he expressed his puzzlement and annoyance at the way in which "continentalism" had become a four-letter word, even for progressives. It certainly was for me and my friends, and Underhill was a chief offender, though I was later to revise my opinion of him.[105]

Political scientist Stephen Azzi, writing of what he calls the "nationalist moment" in English Canada in the late 1960s and early 1970s, draws a suggestive distinction between those nationalists who resisted the influence of the U.S. on Canadian politics, culture, and the economy with moderation, and those who were "visceral" anti-Americans, reacting emotionally against everything associated with the U.S.[106] While this helps to illuminate what he calls the "conjunctural nationalism" of the time—a nationalism resulting from "particular circumstances and events"—I think the differences are better understood in terms of permutations and combinations, which changed with changing circumstances and events, than of distinct categories. Another variation on the theme was what one might call "not-Americanism," the minimalist claim that what defined Canadians was that they were not Americans. A friend and fellow student at the time, Allan Smith, wrote a brilliant scholarly analysis of one expression of this in a comparative study of the use of "melting pot" and "mosaic" as metaphors defining American and Canadian nationality. In adopting the concept of mosaic to describe the pluralism of Canadian culture, nationalists sought to grasp an unavoidable reality, but they also emphatically asserted that it was not American. "American nationalism," Allan wrote, "demands the assimilation of all to a common way; Canadian nationalism, because it has no choice, is predicated upon the toleration of differences."[107] It was easy to slip from "not" to "anti."

I thought my own anti-Americanism was a rational response to American self-centredness and American actions abroad, but there's no doubt that it was visceral at times. Similarly, the Waffle Manifesto of 1969—"For An Independent Socialist Canada"—declared that American corporate capitalism was "the dominant factor shaping Canadian society," and that the American empire was "the central reality for Canadians."[108] The manifesto, which I supported, was a carefully reasoned set of statements and proposals, rooted in a Marxian world view, but there was also no doubt that the "Waffle Movement" was viscerally anti-American on occasion, from its leaders—Mel Watkins, politicized by the Gordon task force, and James Laxer, a young political scientist with deep roots on the left—on down.[109] For nationalists on the left (as Azzi notes) the U.S. was the new Rome, a view open to a variety of expressions.

In a distinction commonly made at the time, Marx*ists*—for whom Marx offered a source of ideological commitment, and not just a set of concepts for understanding the world, as implied by Marx*ian*—often rejected nationalism in favour of a more internationalist stance, though this distinction, too, was not fixed.[110] One instance of its fluidity is offered by a stimulating, and definitely Marxist, essay on the New Left in Ontario by Philip Resnick in a collection published by Black Rose Books in Montreal, which also published the magazine *Our Generation*. I knew Phil, who was a grad student in political economy, and while I never accepted the inevitabilities of Marxism to the extent that he did, I respected his intelligence and integrity, and joined with him in various actions in support of labour radicalism. Intense and articulate in print as well as in person, he argued that the student movement, in pursuing change in education, the "weak link in most advanced capitalist countries," might serve as a catalyst for a wider social transformation, as long as it resisted the temptation of reformism represented by the CCF-NDP in favour of developing a strategy for revolutionary action. While he did not see the American relationship as primary, part of his argument was that "the increasing domination of Ontario universities by American personnel and content [was] a reflection of Canada's colonial relationship to the United States."[111] Nationalism might help to build a revolutionary consciousness.

To be anti-American, in any event, did not mean that one ignored American critics or considered them tainted by their nationality. They were often accused of anti-Americanism in their own country, which is to say that the term was a weapon of rhetorical combat as well as a label for certain positions. Anti-Americanism did not prevent me, or any of my friends, from reading and learning from *The Realist* and the *New York Review of Books*, or *Ramparts* magazine, or other American journals, such as *I. F. Stone's Weekly* or the *Nation*. At the same time, we also read *Canadian Dimension*, which Cy Gonick had founded in Winnipeg in 1963; *This Magazine is About Schools*, founded in 1966 by a group of free school activists in Toronto (Bob Davis, Satu Repo, George Martell); and *The Last Post* from Montreal. The longtime voice of the left, *Canadian Forum*, seemed rather staid by comparison. As time went on, we also followed the emergence of other alternative dailies, weeklies, and monthlies, even if they weren't available in Toronto: *The 4th Estate* in Halifax, the *Mysterious East* in Fredericton, and the

Georgia Straight in Vancouver. The left was localized in its actions but national and international in its politics.

* * * * * *

In the fall of 1967, after completing my comprehensive exams, it occurred to me to investigate ways of visiting the Soviet Union to improve my knowledge of Russian. I still had hopes of teaching Russian history at some point, and possibly of doing comparative research on Russian expansion eastward into Siberia and Canadian expansion west. The idea of a visit turned out to be more complicated than I expected. No Canadian university offered a study program in the Soviet Union, perhaps because there were too many hurdles to jump. In the U.S., however, there were several. The Americans were keener, on the principle of "know thine enemy," and universities worked together to tackle the problems presented by Soviet bureaucracy.

The program offered by Dartmouth College in New Hampshire was very attractive. At its centre was six weeks of intensive language study at the University of Leningrad, followed by two weeks of travel south to Moscow and Tbilisi, then west to Sukhumi and by boat along the Black Sea coast—a cruise!—to Sochi, Yalta, and Odesa. After a few days in Kyiv, students were to fly to Vienna for ten days of free time. At the beginning there were several days of orientation in Helsinki, Finland, and at the end several more of evaluation in Amsterdam. I decided to apply in January. One of my letters of reference had to be from a language instructor, which led me to contact George Melnikov at Carleton, who I was glad to learn actually remembered me and was happy to write on my behalf. Robert McNeal wrote another. I was delighted to receive notice of acceptance at the beginning of March and set about brushing up on my Russian and preparing for what promised to be an exotic adventure. I was not disappointed.

It started with a charter flight from New York to Helsinki in mid-June. I had learned a few weeks earlier that the Dartmouth group of twenty-five students was one of a half dozen or so, from Colorado and Kansas, Georgetown, Michigan State, Oberlin College, and Queens

College of the City University of New York as well. There were 177 of us in all, including group leaders and two program directors who were pretty hard-nosed about relations with our Soviet hosts. The leader of the Dartmouth group was a young professor from Grinnell College in Iowa, not that much older than me, George Young. Self-deprecating, good-humoured, and unpretentious, George was anything but hard-nosed. Searching for him recently on the web, I recognized him immediately in his self-description on the Yale Slavic Languages and Literatures graduate alumni site. I learned that the year after our Russian trip he moved from Grinnell to Dartmouth, where he taught for ten years until his contract expired—"i.e. didn't earn tenure," he adds parenthetically—then moved into business as a dealer in antiques and fine art, later returning to academic work on a part-time basis when the financial pressures of family life eased. He writes that he was probably "one of the few to hold both a Ph.D. in Slavic from Yale and a diploma from the Kansas City School of Auctioneering."[112] This was essence of George. In any event, he was an enjoyable den mother, supervising our activities with a light hand. This also meant that he was no match for our Russian tour guide, Nellie, who pretty much ruled the roost on our tours in and around Leningrad, though she softened over time.

In Otaniemi, just outside Helsinki, we were given placement tests and attended preparatory meetings and seminars. Our time there coincided with summer solstice celebrations, notably Midsummer Eve, which introduced me to the drinking habits of Finns, very similar, as I later learned, to those of Russians. During an evening of excess consumption, I managed to lose my glasses. Fortunately, I had brought along a copy of my prescription, which I was able to fill (with a pair of very heavy horn rims) once we reached Leningrad. The train trip from Finland into the USSR was a bit of an adventure in itself. We had been warned to keep a clear record of the cash, travellers' cheques, and valuables we were carrying, not just because they might be checked on entry, but because a comparison might be made with what we had in our possession when we left. We stopped at the border for customs agents to board, and they spent quite a bit of time checking travel documents and so on. The nervousness they aroused would recur in subsequent encounters with authority, making it difficult to know just where to draw the line between Cold War paranoia, of which I sometimes suspected the program directors, and a realistic judgment of our vulnerability.

We arrived in Leningrad in time for its own midsummer events, the White Nights Festival. The city—St. Petersburg before World War I, then Petrograd, then Leningrad after the death of Vladimir Ilyich Lenin, today St. Petersburg again—was remarkably beautiful at first sight. It exuded "an almost mystical enchantment," in the words of cultural historian Solomon Volkov.[113] Widely known as the Venice of the North, it was laced with waterways and bridges, its streets lined with baroque and neoclassical buildings, many of them designed by the Italian architect Bartolomeo Rastrelli. It had been founded and built on marshlands barely at sea level on the orders of Tsar Peter the Great at the beginning of the eighteenth century. He had wanted both a port for his growing navy and a "window on the west," having travelled in Europe admiring its technology and culture. He achieved both at great cost in human life and labour. The university was located on the Neva River delta, at the historic centre of the city. The Winter Palace, the most famous of Rastrelli's buildings and site of some of the most dramatic events of the revolution, was directly across the river from our dormitory. Kazan Cathedral, the Nevsky Prospect (the main downtown avenue), and St. Isaac's Cathedral were a few blocks beyond. The Peter and Paul Fortress and the Cathedral of Saints Peter and Paul, with its soaring needle spire, were across another branch of the river a short distance away.

Not least impressive about all these buildings was that most of them had been damaged or destroyed in the German siege and blockade of Leningrad during the Second World War and subsequently carefully rebuilt and restored. I'm not sure that any of us stopped to consider the paradox of a communist government, ostensibly oriented toward construction of a new future, devoting such attention and resources to the reconstruction of its imperial past, nor did it occur to us—or at least to me—that *Leningradtsy* might see the history of their city very differently than visitors. For decades after the October Revolution, the pre-revolutionary history of St. Petersburg had faded from view, displaced by the idea of Leningrad as the cradle of the revolution and a centre of industry. In the aftermath of the death of Stalin in 1953 and the onset of the "thaw" in culture and politics that occurred under Nikita Khruschev, this had slowly begun to change. "They started returning us the past," wrote Solomon Volkov, "carefully, unwillingly, a spoonful an hour."[114] I became aware of this only many years later.

We settled into our dormitory on our first day, Sunday, and found our way around the immediate area before attending a concert that night. The dorm rooms were quite large and I shared mine with four other students. It is an indication of the general atmosphere that suspicion of a listening device in the overhead light became a running joke—"Are you there, Ivan?" "Good morning, Ivan." Conditions were rather primitive to a western eye (squat toilets, little or no toilet paper, cold water showers) and otherwise foreign (black bread and kasha for breakfast in the dining hall a short walk across another branch of the river, generally heavy food, and *very* strong sweet tea, made in a large samovar and drunk from a glass in a metal holder). I later bought one of the holders—a *podstakannik*—from an antique dealer. Most of us accepted things for what they were, but others conformed a little too closely to the stereotypical American tourist, complaining incessantly over the following weeks. Whether because of my scepticism about some of their suspicions or just on general principles, I acquired the nickname of *Kanadyets* (the Canadian), always uttered in a mildly ironic tone. I accepted it ironically in return.

On Monday, the first day of classes, there was another language test, which I described in a letter to Marged a couple of days later as "the most traumatic academic experience I've ever had." My Russian was dreadful. I put it down to not having spent enough time "brushing up" in May, but doubtless too many years had passed since my Russian classes at U of A. It was some consolation to realize that I was not the worst in the elementary-level class in which I was placed, but my linguistic shortcomings also made comprehension, much less oral communication, difficult for the next while. Very few Russians spoke any English, and what was I there for, anyway? Nevertheless, it was interesting to spend that Sunday evening at the House of Friendship and Peace, a kind of social centre, I think mainly for young people. Like so many other places we visited, its rooms were formal, with gilt mirrors and chandeliers; it was the former palace of a nobleman before the revolution. The same was true of the Palace of Marriage, which some of us visited a few days later for a wedding. The buildings had become people's palaces. I don't know how I managed at the House of Friendship, where we met some Soviet students. I had my first taste of vodka taken in the Russian style—a shot thrown back all at one go, followed by a gingerale-like chaser. Wisely, I had only one.

Our schedule was hectic in the extreme, at least until we got used to it. There were four and a half hours of classes every morning, including Saturdays, in syntax, phonetics, composition, conversation, and translation. Like so much else, my memory of them is a blur, though I do remember the interest and pleasure of learning about cadence and inflection in spoken Russian, which was a revelation and contributed to whatever confidence I gained over six weeks. Our teacher was very helpful, even if she did treat us as if we were in Grade 3, which in a way I suppose we were. At one point she purchased a 45 r.p.m. record for me from a shop in her neighbourhood, with Yevgeny Yevtushenko reading some of his poetry. This unfortunately disappeared in the mail when I tried to send it home, as did several other things.

Our morning classes were very often followed in the afternoon by a tour of a museum or a visit to a monument in town. One of the most impressive, in a sombre sort of way, was the Piskaryovskoye Memorial Cemetery, where some 500,000 victims of the wartime siege were buried, a little more than half the total. There was no mistaking the central place that the blockade and the war—the Great Patriotic War—occupied in the city's history and memory, either in Nellie's manner or in the vastness of the cemetery itself. The words of a contemporary poet, Olga Berggolts, are carved in a memorial wall: "Here lie the people of Leningrad / Here are the citizens—men, women, children—/ And beside them the soldiers of the Red Army / Who gave their lives / Defending you, Leningrad, / Cradle of the Revolution … Let no one forget / Let nothing be forgotten."[115] The portrait of collective heroism favoured during the Soviet era has only partially survived the opening of the archives since the 1980s, which has revealed the extent of degradation and suffering of Leningraders during the siege, especially non-party civilians. Nevertheless, war, both defensive and aggressive in the name of defence, has played a persistent role in defining Russian identity, whether under the tsars or the Communists, and continues to do so today.[116]

Another visit we made was to the "Bronze Horseman," the equestrian statue of Peter the Great made famous by a poem of Alexander Pushkin. Other trips were by bus to a village or historic site in the surrounding countryside. Later in that first week, we visited Petrodvorets, or Peterhof, the tsar's summer palace about an hour outside of town, and at other times we travelled to Tsarskoe Selo (the Tsar's Village, another imperial estate and more Rastrelli architecture) and further afield to the medieval cities of Novgorod and Pskov. We also had free time, of course, for our own explorations. There were parks everywhere and sites to be seen along the Nevsky Prospect. One of these was the Church of the Saviour on the Spilled Blood, on the Griboyedov Canal, the "spilled blood" being that of Tsar Alexander II, who had liberated the serfs in 1861, but who had also been assassinated—fatally wounded—by a member of Narodnaya Volya, the People's Will, twenty years later. The church had been erected in the tsar's memory, in the distinctively Russian style of numerous cupolas and richly decorated marble, though it had been closed for decades when we saw it and was visibly run down.[117]

Russian specifics aside, the summer served as a general cultural initiation for me. I had never been to the ballet or the opera, and only a few times to the symphony. We went several times to the Kirov Theatre (now the Mariinsky) and were impressed every time by the palatial surroundings, and by the fact that even way up in the cheap seats one was not all that far away from the stage, especially compared to the cavernous O'Keefe Centre in Toronto. And seats in the upper balcony could be purchased very cheaply. From there I saw Mussorgsky's *Boris Godunov*, Prokofiev's *Romeo and Juliet* and *Tale of the Stone Flower*, Rimsky-Korsakov's *Sadko*, and Tchaikovsky's *Swan Lake*. Sets and stage effects were consistently spectacular.

I had never been to a great art gallery, either, my only experience being of the Royal Ontario Museum and the Art Gallery of Ontario, and we visited a few of the best in the world. Foremost among them was the Hermitage Museum, a complex of buildings that included the Winter Palace. We could probably have spent all of our time at the Hermitage and not seen all of its collections. As the St. Petersburg city tourist site puts it today, the three-story palace "boasts 1,786 doors, 1,945 windows and 1,057 elegantly and lavishly decorated halls and rooms."[118] I visited it on the Sunday following the start of classes and reported to Marged that I had managed to take in some of the Italian section—Tintoretto, Botticelli, Da Vinci, Titian—and had only 350 rooms to go. The Hermitage was, and is, especially famous for its collection of French impressionists, acquired by merchants and nobles travelling in western Europe before the revolution. The collection in the Pushkin Museum in Moscow was equally impressive, as we were to discover a few weeks later, and likewise confiscated—or socialized— from wealthy merchants. I had never seen any impressionist paintings in the original, and my mind was pretty much a blank slate when it came to Russian art, which was the focus of the Tretyakov Gallery, also in Moscow. Here, and in the numerous churches we visited (almost all of them museums in the Soviet period), we were exposed to the iconography of the Russian Orthodox tradition. One name only I remember, Andrei Rublev, a late medieval icon painter, perhaps because I later saw the film of the same name by Andrei Tarkovsky.

Whatever else might be said of Soviet conditions, there was no denying that a great many things were accessible to ordinary people. Public transportation seemed to be widely available and heavily used; i.e. packed to the gills. The cost was nominal and based on an honour system. There was no conductor taking tickets; instead, you put a coin in the collection box on the tram and a ticket came out. Sometimes, this required passing your money along to other passengers and receiving your ticket back in the same way, since it was too crowded to make the trip yourself. One suspected that many simply didn't pay, but none of us paid close enough attention to determine whether cheating was common. I don't remember whether the same system was used on the subway. What I remember about the subway was the extraordinary depth of the stations, their lavish decoration, and the recorded conductor's voice over the public address system in preparation for leaving a station: "*Ostorozhno, ostorozhno, dveri zakrivayutsa*"—caution, caution, the doors are closing. Another notable example of cheapness and availability was books. There was an enormous book store on the Nevsky Prospect, Dom Knigi (House of Books), where books were very inexpensive, if also printed on low quality paper and often poorly bound. Russians are a reading people. Whenever a new book, or a new edition of a classic, arrived at Dom Knigi, line-ups immediately formed and the book sold out within hours or days. In another realm entirely, there was ice cream everywhere; it seemed to be the national dish.

At the same time, there was something unmistakably dreary about Leningrad, for all the accessible culture and splendid architecture. It probably didn't help that we had a lot of rain in the first few weeks, but production and distribution of consumer goods—the necessities of food and drink, as well as things like books—was so irregular that line-ups were common at butcher shops, markets, and grocery stores, as well as book shops, when products came in. Otherwise, shelves were often bare. The streets were cleaned by tired-looking elderly women wielding stick brooms. The predominance of women was not because of gender equity in the labour force, but because the male population had been decimated in the Great Patriotic War. Restaurants were dark and unappealing, as I remember them, perhaps because they were often located slightly below ground. The exception was the Astoria Hotel, where admission was restricted to foreigners, except for special cases. On one occasion, I went to the Astoria with two friends I had made, Judson Rosengrant and Lena Lencek, who both later went on to careers in translation and teaching, and another member of the group whose name I don't recall. On our way back to the university, Jud spotted Yevtushenko across the street. He was sure it was him because he had seen him on the cover of *Sports Illustrated* magazine, of all places. We turned and headed back to the hotel and found him at a table on the slightly raised mezzanine level of the restaurant. It was as if a rock star had been seen; Yevtushenko was the rock star of modern Russian poetry, as well as an athlete.[119]

There were also special shops for foreigners, called *beriozka* stores, though locals might shop in them if they had foreign currency. The Soviet Union was hungry for foreign currency and the stores were one means of obtaining it.[120] Individual Soviets sometimes traded rubles for foreign currency at exchange rates much more favourable than the official one, though it was risky to engage in this underground trade. At the *beriozka* stores it was possible to buy high quality luxury goods that were otherwise difficult to obtain, such as amber jewelry, beautifully lacquered boxes (stylized folk images painted on the top), fur hats, and electronics products. Russian friends we made were willing to trade away parts of their libraries for things we might be able to acquire for them at the *beriozka*. I remember one of them looking wistfully at the books he gave me in exchange for my share of the sound system we had bought for him. Another example of this sort of thing was the trade in blue jeans, which were a highly valued commodity among Russians, so much so as to become a kind of currency in themselves. I myself traded for an army belt and buckle, which were somehow appealing at a time when wide belts and buckles had come into fashion in North America. The buckle had an embossed hammer and sickle enclosed in a star.

One Saturday afternoon, I went out to Peterhof for a second time with Jud and Lena and three young Russians whom we had met. In addition to the palaces, fountains, and terraced staircases, there was a large park, not unlike Versailles, which had been its model, where we planned to picnic. We brought along food and drink for everyone, only to discover that our Russian friends had also come prepared, at least with drink for everyone. We found a spot down by the river, where we ate our food and drank some wine, and then had some vodka. The key to this story, however, is not how much we drank but how we drank it. Our friends poured *full* glasses of vodka and offered up a toast, after which we drank the whole thing, followed by lemonade. All was fine for a while, then we had our second drink. At this point my memory fails completely and all that follows I learned subsequently at second hand. We apparently made fools of ourselves for a while, singing and shouting, then caught a bus to the train for Leningrad. At about the third train station I got out. No one stopped me because they thought I was maybe going to be sick. It seems that I leaned on some railing for a while and off went the train. Somehow I found the station master (or he found me), who put me on the next one. When I arrived at our Leningrad station, with the assistance of a kindly Russian soul, everyone had been waiting for about an hour. I was then taken back to the dorm and put to bed. The following morning we went to the Kirov to see Prokofiev's ballet, *The Stone Flower*—Sunday concerts and performances, starting at 11:30 a.m., were part of the Leningrad routine. I wrote home that I was still "pleasantly high," which may partly explain why I thought the performance was the best thing I'd seen, perhaps ever. In any case, it made me very glad to have been introduced to ballet. The following Sunday we went to Tchaikovsky's opera, *Eugene Onegin*.

Our Leningrad program came to an end early in August, marked by closing ceremonies at which we all received certificates from the university. Mine gave rise to general laughter when we saw that my citizenship was given as "USA." An enjoyable banquet followed, and the next day Nellie, our tour guide, very kindly gave me a corrected certificate. We then headed to Moscow by the overnight train, arriving on Sunday morning, 4 August. From now on, we travelled more or less as tourists. We were almost sorry to leave Leningrad, but Moscow turned out to be a whole new world, very much the Big City in comparison—sophisticated, exciting, crowded with people and, at the same time, less of a museum in itself. There was certainly architecture to admire, notably the Kremlin and Saint Basil's Cathedral on Red Square, which everyone had seen in pictures and newscasts, and we visited Zagorsk, just outside the city, one of eight working monasteries in the USSR. There was also official Moscow—a funeral procession for a deceased marshal of the Soviet Army, long line-ups to see Lenin's tomb, which we joined one morning in one of our most off-beat tourist adventures. There he was, like a figure out of Madame Tussaud's. But it was urban Moscow that was most appealing, even though our hotel was on the edge of town, which limited evening ventures into the city centre. The most interesting district we visited was the Arbat, a street of artists and markets that had a bohemian feel. It was here that I purchased my antique tea glass holder. I also visited the Canadian embassy, where I discovered that the postal strike that had begun in mid-July was still on, accounting for the small amount of mail I had received and slowing up mine as well.

Our reaction to Tbilisi was even more enthusiastic. There were very old buildings, some dating back to the fifth century, and narrow winding streets, backed by the Caucasus mountains in the distance, but it was the warm and friendly people—"wild" and "happy," I described them to my mother—that made it seem the most attractive of all the cities we had visited. They were only too happy to engage with us in Russian, and they put on delicious and sociable dinners of shish kebab and Georgian wine. And so began almost a week of relaxation in the far south, the cruise from Sukhumi to Odesa marking a suitable climax to the summer. Odesa seemed a bit flat, by contrast, except for a couple of hours spent visiting the staircase that had featured in Sergei Eisenstein's *Battleship Potemkin*, a famous scene in which a baby carriage tumbled out of control down the stairs as part of a mass flight from marching soldiers, who were killing all before them. It seemed much narrower than it had in the movie, a tribute to Eisenstein's cinematography. Similarly, a few days later, Kyiv aroused little new interest, perhaps because of trip fatigue.

It was in Kyiv, however, late in the afternoon of Wednesday, 22 August, that we learned of the Soviet invasion of Czechoslovakia, putting an end to the Prague Spring. Earlier that day, we had seen truckloads of troops going past our hotel on their way out of town, and before that, on the train at night from Odesa we had seen what appeared to be trainloads of troops and armaments pass by on the neighbouring track. Early on Wednesday afternoon, some of us were taking a boat ride on the Dniepr River, when over the loudspeaker we heard someone declaiming about solidarity with the "Czech brothers" and union against "bourgeois influences." It was only later that we realized that this had been hard core propaganda in support of the invasion, which was repeated on television and in later editions of *Pravda*. I was shocked by this on more than one level; shocked by the invasion itself (its impact would later be felt in Toronto, with the arrival of fleeing Czechs) and dismayed by the fact that I had spent the summer trying to make allowances for the shortcomings of life in the Soviet Union. Shortly thereafter we flew to Vienna, where there were many emigré Czechs, embittered by what had occurred. I was naive enough to be wearing my new Soviet army belt, proud of my acquisition. Fortunately, a man we met gently suggested that it might get me into a little trouble.

Many of my fellow students immediately dispersed to various destinations. A few of us stayed behind and spent the next week or so doing as little as possible. I spent a number of pleasant afternoons with one or two friends, in coffee houses or sipping beer and reading in a pub. Once in the evening (with George, as I recall) we sampled the white wine available in one of the wine gardens in the Vienna Woods on the edge of town. Weiner schnitzel and cordon bleu were choice dinner items. An organ recital in St. Stephen's Cathedral provided entertainment one evening, but otherwise musical Vienna had pretty well shut down. The summer's denouement was spent in Amsterdam and we flew home on 6 September.

Several weeks later, George sent us the results of our oral and written tests in Otaniemi and Amsterdam, roughly tracking our progress. Typically George, he commented wryly that some had done very well, while others "sank to new depths of stark ineptitude in spoken and written Russian," while everyone had gained "something extra-linguistic" over the summer. My own results fortunately fell somewhere in between, the written grade increasing from 58 to 80 and the oral from 1 to 3+ (out of 5). My overall mark was a generous "A," so I had not done too badly. The teacher's comments that he enclosed reminded me of the kinds of things my primary school teachers had written on my report cards, commending my conscientiousness, attentiveness, and so on—always prepared! Looking on the bright side, this perhaps meant that I would have made good progress if I had continued with my Russian studies. As it was, my language skills began to deteriorate soon after my return home, and I never did embark on my comparative research project. The odd phrase stuck with me—*Neechevo nye znaiyu* (I don't know anything)! In any case, it was made clear to me when I interviewed for jobs early in 1970 that no one taught courses outside the field of his or her research. One of the attractions of Mount Saint Vincent later on was that the department was small enough that the modern rules of specialization were overridden by the needs of students, which allowed me to take on the introductory "Western Civ" course and include at least a little Russian history. There was no doubt, however, that George was right about the extra-linguistic value of the summer.

* * * * * *

In the fall, I came back down to earth and work on my doctoral thesis, which I had begun after my comprehensives. I had decided to study the origins of the Hydro-Electric Power Commission of Ontario—Ontario Hydro, as it had long been known. This was partly a result of working at Hydro the summer after my M.A., where I had written a brief history of public utilities in Toronto as part of a long-term project organizing the Hydro archives. The man in charge was Norman Beattie, the head of records management, who had done an M.A. in history at U of T in the 1930s and had a serious interest in the Commission's history. My workmate was Anthony Careless, the son of the historian Maurice Careless and later to become a political scientist himself. We managed to travel to a few Hydro sites in eastern and southern Ontario over the summer as part of our work in the records management offices.

What really drew me to the subject of Hydro, though, was that it was a major example of state ownership in Canada, along with Canadian National Railways (this was long before the creation of Via Rail), Trans-Canada Airlines (before Air Canada and privatization), the Canadian Broadcasting Corporation, and several others. By this time, I was pretty certain that my interests lay in social history. State ownership would not in itself fit into anyone's definition of social history today, but at the time the newly developed field encompassed a wide range of topics. Women's history, for example, was by definition social history, whereas today most people would agree that women's history is an area of study that might be approached in various ways—political, economic, social. Social history, in any event, was code for dissent, even socialism, as well as an approach to the past. Only after I had written my thesis did I see that it was only marginally social in approach; intellectual, yes, technological, institutional, and local, but really very little social history.

The role of the state in the Canadian economy had been debated for many years, and general interpretations had been put forward by leading political economists, including Harold Innis, Alexander Brady, Hugh G. J. Aitken, and, most recently, Gad Horowitz. All of them had explained its relative acceptance in Canada, compared to the U.S., with reference to certain peculiarities of Canadian politics, geography, and culture. For some of them, notably Brady and Aitken, it had been a means of defending Canada against American expansion, while Horowitz saw it as evidence of the distinctiveness of Canadian political culture; tory collectivism, he argued, had given ideological support to state intervention. It was a topic that resonated in the politics of the time.

It was also true, however, that historians had not paid the same attention to it as their colleagues in political economy. This was shortly to change, as I was not the only student to become interested in the subject, or even in Hydro specifically, as I was to learn a few years later when Viv Nelles completed his thesis (later to become a widely admired book) on the triad of forests, mines, and hydro-electric power in Ontario.[121] It was a comment on both the size of the U of T graduate program and the extent to which many of us, our supervisors included, worked away on our own, that I did not become aware of this earlier. Fortunately, we came up with quite different interpretations, though I had to work hard to demonstrate this to Craig Brown. My view, hardly surprisingly, grew in part out of the sources I studied, as well as what I had learned from Marxist political economy and other writing about the state and society. My sources included the journals published by municipal and industry associations, company records, government reports, and the papers of businessmen in southern Ontario that I found in a number of local archives as well as the national archives in Ottawa, the provincial archives in Toronto, and the Hydro archives. I concluded that municipal ownership of utilities was at the heart of the movement for public power and the province's decision to take ownership of transmission lines (and later generating plants), and that provincial action was closely tied to the evolution of electrical technology and its potential for supplanting coal power in manufacturing. Public ownership was the result of the particularities of historical development rather than any peculiar national characteristic, and it was entirely consistent with the dominance otherwise of private ownership. I extended my comparative perspective beyond the U.S. to Britain and Europe and argued that *laissez-faire* was a myth of western capitalism.[122]

It took me eight years to complete my thesis, partly because I took my first job at the University of Victoria in 1970, before I had finished, though it must also be said that many others at the time did so as well and managed to finish more quickly. I followed a few dead ends in pursuit of the social dimension of the public ownership movement, trying to tabulate the characteristics of its participants on the basis of public records of voluntary organizations, local governments, companies, and so on, and it didn't help that I made the mistake of taking a job teaching summer school at U of T after my first year at UVic. I only finished after I had left UVic and returned to Toronto.

Another reason for my slow progress was that I became involved in student politics, whose focus turned particularly to teaching and decision-making in universities in the late sixties, which seemed at least as important as my own research. The box of old documents that I mentioned earlier contains ample evidence of my involvement. There is, for example, a manila envelope of "Graduate History Materials"— announcements, briefs, reports, "working papers," records of meetings, and newsletters of the Graduate History Society (*The Primary Source*!), of which I was an active member. There are articles published by the Canadian Union of Students ("Open Decision Making," "Parallel Structures and Student Power"), others reproduced in other forms (including by gestetner, in those days of primitive technology), and a faded photocopy of a chapter from a book by the psychologist Carl Rogers entitled "Student-Centered Teaching." I particularly remember the last of these, not so much for its specific contents as for the principle enunciated in its title. Many of us supported the idea of student-centred teaching, partly as an approach to pedagogy at both the graduate and undergraduate levels, and partly as a starting point for rethinking the ways in which decisions were made about curriculum and staffing. If students were to play a determining role in their own education, it followed that they should also participate in making decisions about department programs, the courses offered, and who taught them. In fact, we argued that the department ought to be thought of as a community of faculty, staff, and students, and should be structured accordingly to give students a greater—even an equal—voice in decision-making.

Finally, there are copies of three reports that were influential in shaping debates at the time. The first was the report of an advisory committee on undergraduate instruction in Arts and Science, appointed by President Claude Bissell in 1966 and published the following year; then the Commission on University Government (CUG, for short) was established in 1968 and reported in 1969 (in my newsprint version); and finally "The Waterloo Report" on the Americanization—or "de-Canadianization"—of Canadian universities, written by Cyril Byrne, Ken MacKinnon, and Robin Mathews, came out in July 1969. Cyril and Ken were friends with whom I often lunched at a communal table in the Women's Union, just north of Sir Dan. Many of us gathered pretty regularly, including Gerry Friesen and Ann Golden, though Ann had many objections to student radicalism that she did not hesitate to raise. In later years she went on to run the United Way in Toronto and the Conference Board of Canada.

Contemplating all these documents today, I am a little taken aback by their bulk and not at all surprised that the activities they describe absorbed a fair chunk of my time and energy. We went to an awful lot of meetings in the two years from 1968 to 1970, official meetings of committees, caucuses of their student members, "mass" meetings of interested groups. Not in my box of documents but on my bookshelf is a book edited by Howard Adelman and Dennis Lee, *The University Game*. Adelman and Lee were both prominent figures on the left. One of the many meetings I attended was in Adelman's living room, to hear Alexander Cockburn, the left-wing British American writer, who was visiting Toronto and who began his talk by remarking on the similarity of the leftist speech he heard there to what he knew in the U.S., sentences often ending with a strong, argumentative long upward cadence. *The University Game* captures a good sense of the debates of the time—the essays "by turn sober, emotional, provocative, irritating, thoughtful, dogmatic, restrained, shrill," in Claude Bissell's words.[123] They also contain a good dose of the irony characteristic of the time.

Coupled with the irony was a moral critique of the modern university that appealed to my fifties seriousness. In her very fine study of the student movement, Patricia Jasen observes that activists in the liberal arts disciplines—perhaps with the exception of those furthest to the left—were primarily concerned with the wide gap between the rhetoric and reality of their education. Claims that the liberal arts would nurture and develop the imagination, reasoning powers, moral sensitivity, and even the "good taste" of students, bore little relation to the reality of mass education in the multiversity, the goal of which seemed to be preparation for clerical labour in the corporate world. The university expansion that I had experienced since starting out as a student at U of A was driven by a belief in the economic value of the knowledge and "skills" acquired in higher education—"human capital theory"—and an accompanying Cold War belief in the contribution education might make to the defense of the free world. Activists thought that "the university merely contributed to society's problems by suppressing, rather than encouraging, free inquiry and genuine social change."[124] They—we—objected to the dominance of value-free empiricism, the rigidity of disciplinary boundaries, the prevalence of American content (in textbooks, for example), and the neglect of workers, women, and native peoples. Many practical issues arose, notably the role and status of teaching assistants, but time and again we returned to philosophical questions about the purpose of education. Universities, it seemed, served less to free the minds of students than to serve the needs of corporate capitalism.

An institutional expression of this appeared in the report of a History Department committee appointed in late 1967 to "reappraise" the graduate program. Its report declared at the outset that the committee's proposals were related to "what we conceive to be the goal towards which the School [of Graduate Studies] as a whole has been advancing in recent years, i.e. international recognition as the leading Canadian graduate school and one comparable to leading American universities."[125] This competitive intent seemed to many of us a far cry from preparing grad students for their role as instructors in the liberal arts, much less from the ideal of student-centred teaching. The Conacher Report—the committee was chaired by Professor James Conacher—is the first of my "Graduate History Materials" and was a major factor in reorienting the GHS away from its previous focus on social events and the presentation of academic papers to reform in the interests of students.

The committee was also striking for the absence of any grad students in its membership, which made it something of a watershed by the time it made its report in July. Chief among the responses of the GHS in the fall was a call for student participation in any such future committee. In fact, we argued for equal representation with faculty, or "parity," the watchword of the student movement at U of T and elsewhere. Kenneth McNaught, a distinguished senior member of the department, later remarked drily in his memoirs, remembering his own time as an undergraduate in the late 1930s, "Unquestioned was the now exotic assumption that the faculty view of how to best construct a program of study was likely to prove superior to the view of an eighteen year old fresh out of high school."[126] Had he entered U of T as a graduate student, I suspect that he would have said much the same about students in their twenties fresh from their undergraduate degrees. The demand for parity was the point at which McNaught parted company with the student left, with which he otherwise had some sympathy. It was too much a violation of his liberal view of the university. While parity was not an outcome of the student movement in the long term (perhaps for the best), student representation on committees definitely was.

Sometime in the fall I met Mark Phillips, who had just arrived in Toronto with his wife Ruth from Berkeley. It wasn't long before we became good friends, partly because (for me) Mark was such a creative thinker about history and politics, and (for Mark) I served as a way into the politics and history of Canada. We were also temperamentally similar, quiet and serious-minded. It became a running source of amusement that Ruth would come into the front room of their apartment after we had been talking for some time and express surprise that anyone was there, so low were our voices. Our shared interest in teaching and pedagogical reform led to our becoming regulars at meetings of the GHS and being elected to the executive, which meant we helped to formulate the GHS response to the Conacher Report and other matters. One outcome of GHS submissions was that a "Committee of Eight," composed of four faculty and four students, was struck in the fall of 1968 to come up with a departmental response to the Conacher Report.[127]

One thing led to another, and a second committee, also with an equal number of faculty and students, only this time both graduate and undergraduate, was formed in the spring to consider the structure of decision-making in the department—not exactly a "philosophical question," but a prerequisite to pedagogical reform, or so we thought. The "Structure Committee" was appointed in May 1969 and absorbed an enormous amount of time over the following months. John Foster and I were among the grad student members, as were Greg Kealey, a leading member of the undergrad student left, and Craig Heron, who had been in the first tutorial I taught as a graduate TA, among the undergrads. One of its faculty representatives was Harvey Dyck, a thoughtful and approachable professor of Russian history who had replaced Robert McNeal. He took the issues raised by students very seriously, especially our desire to question the purpose of history. On one occasion we invited him to present at an "open forum" on teaching. He arrived with an armload of materials from the Ontario Institute for Studies in Education, which he proceeded to spread over the table where we were all sitting, expecting us to pick them up, just out of curiosity. He was amused when no one did so. Were we not interested in them? Or were we just unfamiliar with the unstructured teaching methods that he preferred? He suggested that the teaching problems that were widespread in the modern university were the result, not so much of poor methods, as of the reluctance of teachers to define their own philosophy of education.[128]

Another faculty member on the committee was Kenneth McNaught, who provided my most memorable moment from the proceedings. At one point, Kealey made an intervention to comment on a point that "Ken" had made. Since I knew he wasn't referring to me—I hadn't made the point—it had to be McNaught, which made it possibly the first time I had heard a fellow student refer to a professor by his first name. The memorable moment came when we were all leaving the meeting after it had adjourned and I overheard McNaught quizzically inquiring of one of his colleagues, "Was he referring to ME?" Here was another indication of the distance we had travelled since the late 1930s. Another moment that I associate with the Structure Committee involved Natalie Davis, then one of only three women in the department and just setting out on a career that would establish her as a leading historian of early modern Europe. Her husband, Chandler Davis, had run into legal troubles in the U.S. as a result of his radicalism and they had emigrated to Canada, Chandler to the U of T mathematics department. The citizenship of faculty members had come up in discussion as a result of the publication not only of "The Waterloo Report" I mentioned above, but also the landmark text in the opposition to Americanization, *The Struggle for Canadian Universities*, edited by Robin Mathews and James Steele.[129] This time I heard Natalie comment to a colleague that she had been discriminated against as a Jew, and discriminated against as a woman, and she was damned if she was going to be discriminated against as an American as well. One had to acknowledge her point.

It may not have been around a Structure Committee meeting that I heard her say this, but at the time of a departmental teach-in that the committee sponsored in early November 1969, which I must have helped organize, since my carbon copy of the announcement was clearly typed on my Olympia portable typewriter. The teach-in drew out the differences in the debate over structure, which focused especially on the question of parity. These differences were real—"polarization" is the word used to describe them in *The Primary Source*—but the striking thing about them, looking back, is that they cut across faculty-student lines.[130] There was opposition to parity within the GHS, and some sympathy for an increased student role among faculty, though not when it came to matters of appointment, promotion, and tenure. A group of faculty (McNaught among them) addressed an open letter to the student newspaper, *The Varsity*, opposing any role for students in staffing decisions, apart from course evaluations, partly because it would undermine the university's quest for pre-eminence by making it difficult to compete for faculty.[131] Those faculty who voiced any support for a student role in staffing, such as Natalie Davis and her friend and colleague, Jill Conway, aroused angry opposition among their senior (male) colleagues. Conway was also among the few who sympathized with the concern about Americanization.[132]

Today, after some forty-plus years teaching at various universities, I can't help wondering how I would have reacted if I had been a faculty member at the time, rather than a student. We were idealists—"utopian" is the word Conway uses—and probably too simple-minded in our criticisms of the department and "the system," which made compromise and politics unlikely in our relations with faculty, even those who were sympathetic. We also shared a characteristic that made many faculty suspicious of power-sharing, which was that we were transient members of the university community. I began applying for jobs in the winter of 1969–70 and did not remain at U of T long enough to see the final outcome of our prolonged committee labours.

Over time, I came to think that, for all the virtues of interdisciplinarity, it should not come at the expense of disciplinary integrity. History had something distinctive to offer as a view of the world. At a "Teaching Day" at Mount Saint Vincent—a day prior to the academic year set aside for profs to discuss questions related to pedagogy, hardly thinkable in 1968—I even found myself on a panel devoted to the question, "Which comes first, content or pedagogy?" responding firmly on the side of content. Forced to choose between getting it right and making it interesting, I said, I came down on the side of getting it right. My idea of a university classroom was one in which students and professors came together in common pursuit of knowledge. As a professor, I invited students into a community of scholarship, and the discipline of history was the common ground on which we met. I've often heard it said that most modern academics pursue careers, not vocations. That may be true, but I, and many of my friends, pursued vocations. I wanted my students to know something when they had finished my course, not just to know where to go to look something up, and not just to be enthusiastic about their subject. These qualities were all well and good, of course, but the end was to know something about their subject, because the cliché was true: the more you know, the more you can learn.

Chapter Seven
Decisions, Decisions

My interview at the University of Victoria early in 1970 went very well, eased by the presence of Charlie Cowan. As I indicated earlier, I was offered a position that I accepted. When I informed the chair of the department at the University of Western Ontario, where I also had an offer, he was clearly surprised that I had chosen UVic over Western, and—who knows?—maybe I would have finished my thesis sooner if I had landed in London, the home of Adam Beck, founder of Ontario Hydro. I had also had an interview at Dalhousie, which was where I was told, when I inquired about the possibility of teaching Russian history, that faculty did not teach outside their specialties, a mark of how much had changed since the 1950s, when almost everyone did so. This was an unsettled period in the Dal history department and it may have been just as well that they turned me down. They also turned down Ken McLaughlin, a former student of Peter Waite's, the senior Canadian historian in the department. Ken went to St. Jerome's College in the University of Waterloo.

Later that spring, in May, Marged and I were married by a very congenial Unitarian minister in our apartment on St. George Street. Mark and Ruth signed the marriage certificate as witnesses. The others who attended were Marged's sister Jane and her former roommate Karen; Ian Lumsden and his wife Nena Hardy, who lived in the apartment below us; Nancy Wildgoose and Don Kubesh, who had married a year earlier and moved to Montreal, where Don taught at Loyola College and Nancy worked as a librarian at Sir George Williams; and Gerry Friesen, who was headed for the University of Manitoba. Rubin was still in Europe and so unable to attend, but he sent us a congratulatory note, pointing out that we were obviously making our relationship respectable before moving to Victoria. This was true. We wanted to get married, but we also thought it would be best if our first impression was not one that required people to accept a violation of one of the major social norms of the time. At the same time, a small domestic wedding without most members of our families, especially our parents, was outside the norm itself.

It was a good decision, as we discovered. Victoria was a socially conservative town, even around the university, where Marged was expected to join a "faculty wives" social group, which she declined to do. One of our first experiences was an evening outing with some friends to the pub at the Oak Bay Beach Hotel—"The Snug"—where I was denied entry because I was wearing jeans, this despite the sports jacket that I also wore. Victoria's claim to be an outpost of Olde England was a tourism gimmick, but it was also an expression of its character. The Empress Hotel on the waterfront was, if anything, even more formal than the Oak Bay Beach, identified above all by afternoon tea in the immense lobby area. My relations with Craig Brown markedly improved after he came out to Victoria to deliver a lecture and we spent an evening together in the Empress bar (I didn't wear jeans). At the end of the evening, he offered to save me from last-minute, late-night prep and give a lecture to my class that met the next morning. Another part of the Victoria social milieu was the requirement of a year's residency in the province before one could be hired in the public library system, which meant that Marged had to wait a year before becoming eligible for a job.

This did not get us off to a great start. The history department was welcoming, however, and there were a number of recently or newly appointed members. In addition to Charlie and Brian, one of them was David Stafford, an Englishman originally from Newcastle who was shortly to make a reputation as a historian of espionage and who became another lifelong friend; another was Ernie Forbes, who later moved on to the University of New Brunswick and became a leading historian of the modern Maritimes. Ernie had a huge library of antiquarian books and government documents on Maritime history in his office, which he had collected because of their scarcity in libraries. These people and others formed a congenial group of colleagues, though it also became apparent that the department had its share of the tensions and divisions that are endemic in universities. Some of these arose from UVic's relatively young age. Founded as a college of McGill in 1903, it later became affiliated with the University of British Columbia and gained its independence only in 1963, which meant that many faculty and administrators were keen to elevate its standards and improve its competitive position, not unlike at U of T. This left one or two old-timers who did not have Ph.D.'s and did little or no research in an anomalous position. The head of the department (as he then was) told all of us newcomers that promotion from lecturer to assistant professor would follow immediately after completion of our Ph.D., and then to associate when we put our first book on his desk.[133]

It didn't help our feeling of belonging that the country experienced a major crisis at the beginning of October, with the kidnapping of the British trade commissioner in Montreal, James Cross, by a cell of the Front de libération du Québec, followed a few days later by the kidnapping (and subsequent murder) of Quebec Labour Minister Pierre Laporte by another cell of the FLQ. The impact of the October Crisis was felt especially in Quebec and Ontario. By mid-month, a state of emergency was declared by the Quebec government and the War Measures Act was invoked by Ottawa.[134] This seemed to some of us an over-reaction, seriously threatening civil liberties. George Bain, the Ottawa columnist for the Toronto *Globe and Mail*, stood out as a critic, as did the federal leader of the NDP, Tommy Douglas, and the political scientist Denis Smith.[135] I even had some sympathy with the goals of the FLQ, if not its methods, and subsequently read Pierre Vallieres' *White Niggers of America*, a famous tract of the times that argued that the position of the Québecois in Canada was akin to that of African Americans in the U.S., and that remedy of the resulting injustices called for extreme action.[136] A few years earlier, René Levesque had left the Liberal party of Quebec to form the Parti Québecois.

I eventually came to think Vallieres' comparison of French Canadians and black Americans grossly exaggerated, and even to think that the War Measures Act had been necessary under the circumstances (reversing the direction of what seems to have been the evolution of majority opinion). What was definitely *un*necessary was the application of the Act to sleepy Victoria, but the president of UVic, Bruce Partridge, denied permission to a radical student group to hold a meeting in one of the university's buildings, supposedly in order to protect the students from possible arrest by the local police. Several of us took part in demonstrations protesting this, as well as the War Measures Act itself, and wrote a letter to President Partridge objecting to his action. My fellow correspondents included Brian, Ernie, Chris Rowe, another young member of the department, Doug Cole, who was visiting from Simon Fraser, and Barrie Ratcliffe, a visitor from England. The Act, we said, was expressly aimed at containing a state of "apprehended insurrection" in Quebec, and there was no need to curtail "free inquiry and free expression" in the university.

The president replied to us at length, arguing that the Act was law across the land and it was the university's duty to uphold the law. The gravity of the exchange was leavened, at least in our view, by the inclusion of each of our ranks in the salutation—four Lecturers and two Visiting Assistant Professors!—which seemed a little too obviously designed to put us in our place, and by the fact that copies were sent to the Dean of Arts and the Head of the Department of History. This was potentially the highlight of my first year at UVic, but more was to come. Later in the term a dispute erupted over the granting of tenure to a member of the English department, the latest of several similar disputes over the previous year. Then, first thing in the new year, the student newspaper, *The Martlet*, revealed serious problems with the president's academic qualifications in a sensational cover story. The top half of the front page contained a copy of a page from *Popular Mechanics*, which included an ad for Blackstone School of Law, just under an ad for the 1965 Electric Eye Insect Trap. The lower half had a page from an article found at the university's counselling service, with the heading "Beware the Degree Mill!" Part way down the first column appeared the Blackstone School of Law. Running across the bottom were the words, "Guess What? see back page." On the back was a picture of

Bruce Partridge and the information that he had received not only a Bachelor of Laws from Blackstone, but a Doctor of Jurisprudence.[137] Partridge, who also had a B.A. from Oberlin College, resigned a few months into the following academic year, in November 1971, and later went on to acquire a more reputable law degree at UBC. Friends and students aside, I began to wonder whether I had made the right career choice in going to Victoria.

My reaction to the War Measures Act is one indication that I didn't leave my politics behind when I ceased being a student and joined the ranks of faculty, nor did any of us. I became involved in the local NDP, if only marginally, at the encouragement of Barry Askinas, a member of the anthropology department. We once attended a riding association meeting where Tommy Douglas came to speak, fully living up to his reputation for rousing oratory. The most striking thing about the meeting, however, was that Barry and I seemed to be at least thirty years younger than anyone else. Victoria was not a centre of NDP activism, or youth activism in general. The possibility of change was in the air, though, with the approach of the 1972 provincial election, and Barry tried to persuade me to run for the local nomination. The fact that I was a total newcomer and not yet even a member is an indication of the semi-moribund state of local organization, but that he brought up the possibility at all is also a sign of the radical times. I declined, I think partly because I was already thinking of leaving, but the party went on to win the election under the leadership of Dave Barrett.

The NDP victory is evidence of the continuity of sixties radicalism beyond the 1960s, but also of the variability of "the sixties" as a coherent historical moment. At about the same time as BC was going NDP, the Ontario party, led by Stephen Lewis, was expelling the Waffle movement from its ranks. This was as good a benchmark as any for the end of my "sixties," partly because my support of the Waffle was Ontario-centred, due to the people I knew—Mel Watkins came out to Victoria to give a couple of lectures at one point and I acted as his host—and partly because I handed in my letter of resignation to Toby Jackman, the acting head of the history department, in the spring of 1972. After some serious thought, Marged and I had decided that we would find it more worthwhile to try our luck back in Toronto than to continue with the frustrations of Victoria. We talked about it at length, both between ourselves and with others, including Donald and Nancy. Don had taken a job at UBC at the same time as I had taken mine at UVic, and he and Nancy came over to Victoria often to visit his parents, who had retired to Victoria from their farm outside Beausejour, Manitoba. Conversations between us were often about our unhappiness in our jobs. Donald's interest in aboriginal issues continued to grow, and he found himself out of step with most of his colleagues. He too decided to resign, return to Montreal, and go into law. No discouragement of my own thoughts about moving came from his direction.

Dinners with him and Nancy and his parents were among the pleasures of our time in Victoria. His mother, Mary—known to us all as Mariushka—was an excellent cook and a warm and hospitable host, and Marged and I spent some very enjoyable evenings with them all, dining and joining in singalongs, on one occasion staying overnight. Some of our other contacts were equally enjoyable, including evenings and other times spent with Charlie, his wife Lorraine and their children, and with Brian and Donna Dippie. Charlie and Lorraine had put us up when we first arrived, until we could find an apartment, which we actually did fairly quickly, in a magnificent old converted mansion on Rockland Avenue in the older part of the city. During our second year, Terry Copp came to UVic from Loyola as a visiting professor and we got to know him and his wife Linda and their children, Reuel and Monica. Terry injected life into the department, stimulating intellectual debate, as well as organizing touch football games between faculty and students on Saturday mornings and occasional poker games among the faculty. We got to know each other well enough that Linda confided before they left that she was pregnant, and would in time give birth to a second son, Robin.

* * * * * *

Despite the pleasures, we headed back to Toronto in the summer of 1972 with a mind to take stock of our future. I wanted to finish my dissertation—I wasn't ready to leave history entirely, like Donald—and to think about the possibility of opening a bookstore. Bookselling offered the possibility of combining intellectual work with independence, and I soon began thinking about it seriously. I found a part-time job at the University of Toronto Bookstore while I was completing my thesis, serving a kind of apprenticeship under David Stimpson, bookman *par excellence*, whom I had met earlier through Ian Lumsden. David was then manager of the store and would later become a sales rep for several university presses. When he retired a few years ago, his friend and colleague John Eklund wrote of him that he was "always conscious of our sometimes conflicting obligations to publisher, bookseller, author, reader, and the book itself."[138] I imbibed a version of that, including the last on the list, never delivered as a sermon but embodied in practice.

Over the next couple of years, Marged and I travelled the roads of southern Ontario, scouting out possible locations for a bookstore. I remember the dismay we felt in St. Catharines, standing on the curb of a one-way downtown thoroughfare and wondering how many drivers slowed down, much less stopped. (The city restored conventional two-way streets a quarter-century later.) Other places had little downtown to speak of, in the sense of a place where people might actually walk from shop to shop. Malls were taking over and I wasn't interested in locating in a mall. In the meantime, we also travelled to Montreal to visit both Don and Nancy and Terry and Linda, where conversation turned occasionally to the possibility of finding a place where we all might live together. After a time, Don and Nancy opted out, and talk with Terry and Linda became more serious after Terry took a job at Wilfrid Laurier University in Waterloo. Our thinking about a bookstore location took on a new focus when we decided to set up house jointly with them and their children. Now the search for a business location was combined with a search for a place to live.

On a visit Terry made to scout out the possibilities, we made a series of rough concentric semi-circles northeast of Kitchener-Waterloo and happened on the village of Elora, less with the idea of assessing its bookstore possibilities than of getting a cup of coffee. I didn't really know Elora, except by reputation, which included reports of local conflict over a plan to build a new bridge over the Grand River. Marged and I had made trips into the country west of Toronto, but usually only as far as Caledon, Belfountain, and the "Forks of the Credit," which were destinations for anyone interested in the historic countryside of southern Ontario. I think Tone Careless and I may have paid a visit on one of our Hydro-related excursions. In any event, by every rule of bookselling that I had read, Elora's population (then about 2500) was far too small to support a bookstore, which was thought to require a local market of at least 20,000. Even at that, one might need to combine books with stationery. This was also the advice of Beth Appeldoorn, co-owner of the famous Longhouse Bookshop, the pioneering venture in the exclusive sale of Canadian books that had opened a few years earlier on Yonge Street in Toronto. She was very encouraging (as she and her partner, Susan Sandler, were to authors as well), but she thought the undeveloped state of the Canadian book trade called for caution. She even thought it might be worth installing a rack of Harlequin romances, in the interests of steady trade.

Idly inquiring about space for rent on Mill Street, which ran along the Grand River, we learned that there wasn't any, but that the owner of The Yarn Bird, a wool store, might be willing to rent the storage space adjoining her store. This turned out to be a stroke of good fortune. The owner, Eileen Pedersen, wasn't sure the space—somewhat cramped, with no street frontage other than the front door—was suitable, but she would consider subletting if I was interested. Once I had got past the clutter of storage, it seemed possible that the disadvantage of the space's dimensions for some retail purposes might be ideal for books. It was long and narrow—lots of wall in proportion to floor space! One wall stretched forty feet from front to back, the other somewhat shorter because of the staircase to the second floor and the door into the Yarn Bird. The width was a little under nine feet, enough room for a low display row down the centre. The front door had a large window, and part of the entryway could be made into display and storage space. A filing cabinet and check-out desk might fit nicely in the area under the staircase.

Two things made it worth seriously considering. One was that Elora was no ordinary small town. Situated at the upriver end of the Elora

Gorge, it had been a tourist destination since the mid-nineteenth century. The falls that traced the descent of the river, joining up with Irvine Creek (and its own gorge), were picturesque and romantic—small rocky islet in the middle, dividing the flow—and had provided power for a large flour and grist mill and a number of small manufacturers. These all had gone into decline in the course of the twentieth century, and the population along with them. The resulting fall in property values had made it possible for artists and artisans to establish themselves relatively cheaply in recent years, along with craft retailers, antique dealers, restauranteurs, and developers. The old mill was in the process of being renovated, with a view to opening as an inn.

One of the earliest of the craftspeople—maybe the first—had been Nancy and Peter Knudstrup. Peter had trained as a potter in his native Denmark. Looking for a place to open a studio and shop in 1969, Nancy had come across an ad in the *Globe and Mail* real estate section for an old Presbyterian Church in Elora, which had been unused for many years and was deconsecrated.[139] They bought it and moved in. Fred Thompson, an architect who lived in the village and taught at the University of Waterloo, acquired and renovated a building on Mill Street down from Eileen's store and created shops on the main floor. Clare and Helen Claus, who had had a craft shop in the old Gerrard Street Village in Toronto, moved their business to one of these spaces. Bernard Minarovich had opened an antiques store next to Eileen's, as did Catherine Dickinson further down the street. All of these people later became friends, especially Eileen. By our time, the village had become a new kind of tourist destination, and the number of weekend visitors from Kitchener-Waterloo, Guelph, Hamilton, Toronto, and places in between dwarfed the local population.

The other thing the location had in its favour was low overhead. Basically, this was the result of modest rent for a space that was both small and excess to Eileen's needs, and my capital requirements were also small. I could manage renovations, decorating, and shelf-building myself, with a little help from my friends. At a time when cash and cheques were the normal mode of transaction, and inventory control was a matter of keeping up-to-date file cards, there was little need to purchase a sophisticated cash register or accompanying accounting system, certainly for the scale of operation I was contemplating. All that remained was the purchase of lighting fixtures, a store sign, office supplies, and inventory. Bookselling on a shoestring just might be workable in Elora. Our discovery of a house in the country nearby, near Alma, to which an ell wing could be added to make a kind of rural duplex, decided the matter.

It is remarkable to me, looking back, how simple it was to get going, compared to what a similar venture would entail today. Actually, the likelihood of its being done at all today is small. There were no big-box retailers then, discounting new books for quick turnover, not to mention competition from the World Wide Web or e-books. The business was more highly structured—retail book prices were fixed, while the discount one received from publishers and distributors was generally the same, whatever one's size. A lot of excitement surrounded the book trade in Canada, for all of Beth Appeldoorn's wise cautionary advice, and despite the assessment of the report of the Ontario Royal Commission on Book Publishing in 1973 that it was in a "pitifully underdeveloped condition."[140] Longhouse, A Different Drummer Books in Burlington, the Book Shelf of Guelph, and Bookmark in Charlottetown were examples of vibrant stores that opened in the early 1970s, joining the somewhat older Book Cellar in Toronto (1961), Munro's in Victoria (1963), Hurtig's in Edmonton (1956), and Duthie's in Vancouver (1957). Britnell's in Toronto and the Book Room in Halifax were ancient by comparison. Independent bookselling seemed to have a future.

One reason for this was the rise of paperback books—Miss Fraser's handout again!—which had been coming into their own over the previous decade or so. The flowering of Canadian writing and publishing in the aftermath of the Massey Commission and the creation of the Canada Council played a key role, though the literary historian Nick Mount has since questioned this, arguing instead for the importance of increased affluence and education.[141] The national self-discovery that showed itself in such ventures as the New Canadian Library, the Carleton Library series, and the journal *Canadian Literature*, and in books like W. L. Morton's *The Canadian Identity*, George Grant's *Lament for a Nation*, and Margaret Atwood's *Survival* also played a role. Domestic publishers grew in number, despite recurring conditions of crisis: Coach House (1965), Anansi (1967), Lorimer (1968), and Women's Press (1972) in Toronto, for example; Oberon (1966) in Ottawa, Tundra (1967) in Montreal, Hurtig (1967) in Edmonton, Douglas and McIntyre (1971) in Vancouver, Breakwater (1973) in St. John's, and Porcupine's Quill (1974) in Erin, not far from Elora. The backlists of larger houses, such as McClelland and Stewart, Fitzhenry and Whiteside (Fitz and Witz in the trade), Clarke Irwin, Thomas Allen, Macmillan, and the university presses rapidly expanded.

Few of the new stores were devoted entirely to Canadian books, but many displayed them prominently, as I planned to do. My idea was to have a general bookstore, but to follow my own tastes and interests, at least in the beginning, with strengths in literature and history. At the rear of the space on Mill Street, overlooking the river, there was a section marked off by a partial divider, where I planned to have a good selection of children's books. Judy Sarick, a former children's librarian, had opened the Children's Bookstore in Toronto in 1974 with her husband, giving children's books a profile they hadn't had before and setting a high standard in the quality of her stock. She was later a member of a children's book panel that occasionally met on CBC's *Morningside*, hosted by Peter Gzowski, another means by which books achieved a presence in the culture of the time.

I set to work getting the space ready. Taking a cue from Different Drummer, I gave the shelves bright colours against white walls. Later, I was suitably gratified when Al Cummings, owner of the Burlington store, dropped by after I opened and pronounced judgment: "Very crisp," he said. Less crisp was my improvised use of adjustable shelving hardware. Designed to make the shelves level, I installed it in such a way that shelves tilted slightly backward so that books facing out would not fall forward. It worked reasonably well in the end. We chose a name, "elorabooks"—one word, letters all in lower case. This worked nicely as an identifier, but it turned out to be too clever by half when it came to the phone book. By the rules used by Ma Bell, the single word took the name out of alphabetical order and put it at the end of all the entries beginning "Elora." The next year, the name, for phone book purposes, became "Elora Books."

I also began writing and visiting publishing houses to open accounts. Most of them were very accommodating, especially those with whom I could make some personal contact. My account was going to be a small one by any standard. To have any depth in my stock I had to be able to order single copies, which was not unusual except in the proportion of my orders they would make up. And if I ordered in quantity, it would be in threes, fives, and maybe tens. Since I was only an hour or so's drive from my major suppliers, I planned to pick up orders regularly by car, which would avoid the need to stock a season's worth of individual titles, as well as offering some insurance against buying too few copies if a title happened to do better than I expected.

Doing most of this myself—ordering, receiving, shelving, selling—meant that I knew pretty well every title in the shop, which was immensely useful in fielding inquiries or making recommendations to customers. I also did a lot of reading, extending my literary horizons to include genres with which I had only passing familiarity, the vast realm of children's literature in particular. As had been the case in my previous academic life, reading was both work and pleasure. It is a truism of the book trade that the success of any independent bookstore rests on the knowledge of its staff and their ability both to answer the needs of their customers and to communicate their own interest and pleasure in their reading. The staff in my case consisted mainly of me, assisted by Marged on weekends and occasional part-time help, notably an engaging young man not long out of high school, Lyn Vasey. Unlike academic life, one could measure a part of one's success in concrete terms, in the tally of daily sales.

When the store finally opened in August, it received a nice notice in the *Fergus-Elora News Express*, sending readers to the new store "squeezed between the Yarn Bird and Bernard's Antiques." Bryan Hayter, the *News-Express* reporter, had paid us a visit soon after our sign went up. Before long, word spread and customers began coming through the door. I soon came to realize that, despite its small population, there was a sizeable reading public in Elora and its immediate environs—Salem to the north, Fergus to the east, and the surrounding countryside. It also became apparent that there were two kinds of "tourists": regular visitors from nearby, especially Guelph and Kitchener-Waterloo, and those who came more occasionally from further afield. I learned that there was nothing like doing business in a small town for getting to know one's neighbours. Daily treks to the post office to pick up the mail, coffee at the Iroquois Hotel or Floriel's restaurant on Mill Street, trips to the bank to deposit one's earnings: these all involved personal encounters even before I had opened my door for the day.

One result of these personal contacts was that I soon became involved in organizing local events, though I avoided clubs like the Optimists, for better or worse. One of the most enjoyable events was the Elora Heritage Festival, a winter carnival held every year at the beginning of February. By 1978 I was chair of the organizing committee, working with people like Nancy Knudstrup and Ellen Melville, a free spirit who occasionally dropped into the bookstore and was much involved in the local arts community. The festival featured a snow sculpture contest, a broomball tournament, cross-country skiing, and other outdoor activities, as well as a variety of programs in the community hall.

The other organization I became involved in, on a much larger scale, was the founding committee of the Three Centuries Festival, an early music series that was the brainchild of Michael Purves-Smith, a member of the faculty of music at Wilfrid Laurier. Sometime in 1979 I received a call from Merrick Jarrett, a pioneer of Canadian folk music who lived in the area and worked for the Kitchener Public Library. Merrick was a warm, down-to-earth man who frequented the bookstore with his wife Mary, and who had put in quite a few hours in our first year helping us clean up smoke damage after a small fire had broken out overnight in Eileen's store. I don't recall what his connection with Michael was, but he asked if I was interested in helping to mount the proposed festival. I became a member of the board of directors as a result and ended up organizing a juried art show at the Wellington

County Museum as an added attraction. The festival was a great success in its first year, 1980, and continues to operate as the Elora Festival, long ago having abandoned the idea of specializing in music from the sixteenth to the eighteenth centuries.

The two festivals involved different but overlapping groups of people, a sign, I thought, that the village divisions of the early seventies were perhaps beginning to heal. Those divisions arose from conflict over the building of two low-rise apartment blocks not far from the uptown business district. The village council gave its approval, but a citizens group formed in opposition, concerned that the wrong kind of development would damage the nineteenth-century character of the village. It quickly became apparent that the opposition was chiefly made up of residents fairly new to the village—migrants from the big city seeking peace and quiet—while the defenders were longtime Elorans. Divisions worsened when plans were announced for a new bridge that would cross the gorge on the edge of town. Both issues divided people roughly along "quality of life" vs. "economic development" lines. Opponents of the bridge project saw it as a threat to the natural environment of the gorge, while those in favour liked the idea of highway traffic being diverted away from the main street to the edge of the village. In the end, both the apartment buildings and new bridge went ahead, but not before relations between newcomers and oldtimers became embittered, even between those who were not directly involved in decision-making.[142] Participation in the winter carnival came largely, though not exclusively, from the "oldtimer" part of the community, while the music festival was aimed especially at newcomers and visitors. For many of those involved, however, both events aimed to bring together everyone in the village and they achieved some success.

My approach to bookselling was embedded in its time. It was a business, to be sure, but it also had an educational function. One served as a kind of cultural mediator, no less than a magazine or book reviewer, hoping to select books that met people's tastes and needs but that also opened up possibilities and opportunities for them. Some booksellers were downright missionaries for a cause, like Beth Appeldoorn, while others served a special need, like Bob Miller of the Bob Miller

Bookroom in Toronto (and previously of the SCM Bookroom), whose selection of scholarly books not only responded to professors' special demands for course books at the University of Toronto, but sustained many a grad student hungry for the latest monograph in his or her field. The same was true of David Stimpson at the U of T Bookstore. Serving a "market" was secondary to, or at least equal with, a commitment to cultural service, even cultural improvement—Victorian as this might sound—in the same way that the CBC, or intellectuals, or even political parties (acting in a manner true to their roots) thought of democracy as a "raising up" of the people rather than a levelling down to the lowest common denominator. It was its own form of idealism, combined with a sense of duty and a measure of scepticism.

Little of this ethic remains today, for better or for worse. Instead, the purchase of a book is a highly individuated transaction, as is tuning in to a radio program, or voting. There are exceptions, of course. The independent bookstores that survive continue to serve their customers and their books, but there is little to differentiate the large chains and online retailers from their counterparts dealing in other products. I'm not even sure that "bookman" (or "bookwoman"), and the roundedness it implies, is a term that continues to be used.

Over the five years that I owned it, the store expanded to include a small section of Canadian magazines, some children's records (these were the years when Raffi, Fred Penner, and Sharon, Lois and Bram transformed children's music), book plates, road maps, and calendars. Sales grew annually, exceeding the averages for American bookstores with sales under $50,000 (as reported in an American Booksellers Association survey of 1977) in sales per square foot, turnover, and earnings.[143] Even so, earnings were not enough to support a family. Megan was born in 1977 and Helen in 1979, and Marged left her job as a librarian at the University of Waterloo for the time being to look after them. This meant a significant drop in our income. I had also been teaching courses part-time for Wilfrid Laurier and Waterloo, which I would not be able to continue if I increased store hours in an effort to expand sales.

The small size of the store, in any case, placed a limit on potential total sales. When a small building a few doors down on Mill Street came on the market, we tried to buy it, but the asking price was out of our reach. This was only one early sign of how the success of an arts and crafts community like Elora's was almost self-defeating. Real estate buyers with an eye on profits from turnover, as well as property developers who required a return on their investments in improvements, threatened to price the artists and craftspeople (who had been the basis of growth in the first place) out of the market. The owner of the building we were interested in made a point of saying, with pride in his own shrewd assessment of property values, that one only made serious money with the initial transaction in a rising real estate market like Elora's.

The result for me was that I returned to academic life. What turned out to be an interlude in the book trade had two specific benefits, besides the friendships I had made and the pleasures I had enjoyed. One was that I returned to university inoculated by my time in the "real world" against the inward gaze that is the chief occupational hazard of academic work. Looking back, I also think my immersion in business and in the life of a small community moderated my politics. The demands of meeting a bottom line and serving customers, and of participating in organizing committees that drew on a wide range of personalities and resources showed how important it is to understand another point of view, to negotiate, and to compromise in arriving at solutions to problems. (The time I spent reading children's books rather than political tracts must also have made a difference!) I still thought of myself as on the left, but I became less of a radical and more of a "progressive," to use the rather vague term that now describes much of the modern, watered-down left.

The other benefit was that I had become acquainted with a figure prominent in the history of Elora, a nineteenth-century journalist, businessman, and politician named Charles Clarke, whose influence had extended beyond the village to the province of Canada and later Ontario. His portrait hung in the reading room of the local Carnegie public library and was impossible to miss, and some of his papers were held at the Wellington County Archives on the road to Fergus. He became the focus of much of my research and a resulting book.[144]

I discovered, among other things, that he had once noted in his diary that Elora was ready for a good bookstore if one were opened by a "pushing, enterprising man ... an intelligent fellow knowing the difference between 10 cent rubbish and a good novel or other book." I had never thought of myself as particularly "pushing," but I was lucky to discover that Elora still fit Clarke's description a hundred years or so later.

* * * * * *

I took a one-year term position in the history department at Wilfrid Laurier, then applied for the Marston LaFrance Fellowship at Carleton University in Ottawa. In those days, it had two parts, one a research fellowship available to a member of Carleton faculty, the other a post-doctoral teaching fellowship, designed essentially to replace the person awarded the research fellowship. I thought my chances were pretty slim. By 1981, I was six years past completion of my doctorate, well past normal eligibility, and ownership of a bookstore in the intervening years would not normally have helped. The qualifications were generously stretched almost certainly because of Mark Phillips, who had won the research half and told me about the teaching half. In any event, I had the good fortune to win. We packed up and moved to Ottawa for the year, in the process leaving Terry and Linda behind, and living beside the unknown couple who rented our half of the house. Fortunately, our friendship with them survived this abandonment.

The year was productive on various fronts. It was a pleasure to be in Ottawa and to spend time with Mark and Ruth and their children, Sarah and Emma, who got along well with Megan and Helen. It was also a pleasure to get back into teaching in a serious way, particularly in a class focused on reading books and discussing them in a tutorial setting with a small number of students. The books I chose were all short studies that served as entry points into their times, connected by lectures (mine) that surveyed the intervening periods, not unlike my own introductory course in European history at the University of Alberta. I particularly remember the first, *Heloise and Abelard* by Etienne Gilson, at once a dual biography of two remarkable individuals, an absorbing love story, and a cultural history of the High Middle Ages. It served as a prefatory introduction to the main body of the course, "Turning Points in Modern History." I also got to know members of the Carleton faculty, especially Blair Neatby, a friend of Mark's and one of the leading Canadian historians of the time, author of the standard biography of William Lyon Mackenzie King. Many years later, he offered critical support for my intellectual biography of his doctoral supervisor and mentor, Frank Underhill. Two others I especially remember were Keith Johnson, an eminent historian of Upper Canada, and Naomi Griffiths, the leading English language historian of the Acadians, who was then Dean of Arts at Carleton, the first woman to hold the position.

At the end of that year, in a very tight job market, I was lucky enough to get an appointment at Mount Saint Vincent and we were off to a part of the country we hardly knew. My liberally designated "post-doctoral" year at Carleton helped to get me to the Mount, as I learned some time later. One of my new colleagues was Frances Early, an American historian who later achieved her own eminence as a women's historian. She had arrived at the Mount the year before and knew someone in the Carleton history department who apparently gave a little additional oomph to my letters of reference. One attraction of the position was that it took us to one of the most historically interesting cities in the country, though it would be hard to claim that now, when much of downtown Halifax has recently been demolished to make way for splashy modern buildings.

I knew almost nothing about the Mount when I applied for the position, which was one of a number of history openings advertised in Canada in 1982, all of which I applied for, most unsuccessfully. I don't think I had known of the Mount's existence until the year before, when I had stayed in the University of King's College residence for the Learned Societies Conference, which was at Dalhousie. Waiting to check in, I heard the person ahead of me ask the young woman at the desk if she was a student at King's. The young woman said no, she was at Dal, but she was transferring to Mount Saint Vincent in the fall because it was smaller than Dal. I was startled by this. Albertan by origin,

Upper Canadian and British Columbian by temporary residence, I did not think Dal was all that large. This was not, as it turned out, the last time I was to hear about the small size of the Mount.

I didn't really know what to make of the Mount on my first encounter, nor, for that matter, for a couple of years afterwards. My interview went well enough, though I did feel some disquiet when I was shown around the library, which was then housed in the north wing of Evaristus Hall, where Math and Computer Science and Women in Science and Engineering are now located. It was rather attractive, classically a "library": lots of dark wood, ceiling two stories above the main floor reading room, the second story a mezzanine level, including a periodicals reading area at one end. My impression of the Canadian history collection, however—very rough, of course, and no doubt exaggerated—was that its size was only somewhat larger than my own, comprising books that were if anything somewhat older. Meanwhile, the offices in Seton Academic Centre, the main Arts building, were spacious, but oddly fitted out with cupboards and closets, while a single bookcase, perhaps four feet high by six feet long, seemed to be the standard issue. I wondered what these two things together might portend. And while the department was welcoming and friendly—dinner at Satisfaction Feast, a local vegetarian restaurant—I thought (not really being sure whether I imagined it) that I detected an undercurrent of uneasiness. I put it down to the fact that my rival for the advertised vacancy was an internal candidate, about whom there might naturally be divided feelings.

Nevertheless, I was very pleased to be offered an appointment by the Dean of Humanities, Sister Patricia Mullins, a chemist and member of the religious order that had founded the Mount a hundred years or so earlier, the Sisters of Charity of St. Vincent de Paul. The order had first come to Halifax from New York in 1849 and embarked on a variety of missions related to teaching, health care and social work. At its founding in 1873, the Mount was an academy designed to train sisters and novices as teachers. Over time, it broadened its admission policies to include other young women, and in 1925 it secured a charter as a college from the Nova Scotia government, becoming the only independent women's college in the British Commonwealth.[145] I only gradually became familiar with its history and traditions, which were both a source of pride to faculty, staff and students, and something of a burden, with all of the rules and hierarchy they brought with them.

Marged and I and the children arrived in Halifax at the end of July and bought a house. Just how we did so is a story in itself. The owner was a member of the Mount faculty and I had already heard of the house's availability. We offered to rent, the owner agreed, and we went off looking forward to an unexpected period of relaxation. Then the owner told us she had a party who would rent with a promise to buy in a year's time, which sent us back onto the rental market. Rents striking us as unusually high, we returned to the owner and offered to buy immediately. I don't know what happened to the other potential rental-purchasers but we still live in the same house. I set to work moving into my office and getting to know the institution I expected to spend some years in, maybe even a career. In those days, there were regular meetings of the entire university faculty, at which attendance was mandatory. The first of these I attended was a year-opening meeting in the Multi-Purpose Room in the Rosaria Student Centre, where members of the administration harangued us—existing faculty as well as new—about various matters, for the better part of a morning. The main theme that I remember, perhaps because I heard it so often thereafter, was the university's straitened financial circumstances.

The *person* I chiefly remember was the President, Margaret Fulton, who had some strange ideas about university administration, but who also had a pretty clear idea of what universities were for, especially this particular university. Margaret, who was the first lay president of the Mount, made no secret of her feminism, either inside or outside the university, and, at least to all outward appearances, was unconcerned by the feathers she inevitably ruffled. If anything, she revelled in it. She was a bit of a force of nature, a Big Lady feminist who served the cause not so much by theorizing or propounding a particular point of view or ideological line as simply by speaking up for women's right to be heard, and to govern, in all spheres of activity, equally with men. As president of the Mount, heir to the mantle of Sister Catherine Wallace, who had put the university on the national map (even if I hadn't noticed it), Margaret acquired a pulpit and she did not hesitate to use it. She aroused opposition because she said outrageous things, and because she tended to take advice from a small coterie of friends, but no president since, with one or two exceptions, has been as willing (or perhaps as able) to articulate a vision for the university to which a significant number of academic staff could commit themselves as an ideal to be pursued.

Margaret could not, of course, have pursued her vision alone. In particular, she could not have led the Mount into its post-ecclesiastical era without the assistance of Walter Shelton, who had come to the Mount before her as Dean, when the Dean was the single senior academic administrator, and had become Vice-President (Academic) after an administrative reorganization. Margaret was President during most of his term as AVP, and the two of them made a decidedly odd couple. Walter was no feminist; on the contrary, he was a distinctively English male chauvinist and capable of a domineering attitude as offensive to many women as Margaret's feminism was to many men. I have no idea, in fact, how he came to be appointed Dean in the first place. I can only guess that those responsible recognized the qualities that made him the shrewd and innovative administrator that he in fact became. Margaret and he were not close, but they had a very good working relationship; they saw how they could be useful to each other and they found ways of working together, at least for a time—Margaret the visionary, Walter the down-to-earth realist. He also, in fact, played no small role in securing Margaret's initial appointment, something that might serve as a cautionary lesson in drawing too simple a connection between attitude and action. By the time I arrived, at any rate, his term was over, and he did not re-offer, probably because he knew his reappointment would have been contested. One minor result of his term, however (among many major ones), was that Margaret's eccentric ideas of administration by "quality circles" that I heard at my first faculty meeting remained on the drawing table.

The idea of a generation, or cohort, applies to the history of institutions just as it does to the history of ideas and social relations. At least, from my narrow little perch in the Department of History I could see generations around me, defined not so much by age as by time of appointment to the university faculty. Frances and I were members of the same generation, appointed within a year of each other, and to no small degree as a result of a concerted effort initiated by Walter to ensure that faculty were appointed only on the basis of their academic qualifications. In the past, it had not been uncommon for faculty members to be appointed because their spouses had been appointed at Dal, and someone at Dal had called someone at the Mount to arrange a convenient dual appointment. While in many cases this worked to the Mount's advantage, it also perpetuated a kind of junior status, as well as being procedurally dubious. Others of my generation whom I particularly recall from the time were Barnett Richling, in the Department of Sociology and Anthropology, and Susan Drain from the English department, who were both at my lunch table on that opening day of inspirational and cautionary talks from administration.

My next-door office neighbour, Pierre Payer, was a member of an earlier cohort. Pierre was a philosopher, as I noted earlier, though as much a historian in his field of research, which was the theory and practice of confession in the medieval church, and its role in the regulation of sex and sexuality, in which he was one of the leading authorities in the English language. He was never recognized as such at his own university, an indication of how personalities and personal histories deform reputation and standing in academic life. Pierre was also a priest and chaplain of the university, as well as professor, when he was first appointed, but he had since left the priesthood and married a former nun. We spoke often of the university in all its dimensions and how it had changed in so many of them in only twenty or so years. Before the construction of Seton Academic Centre, the entire faculty had been housed in Evaristus Hall, not in offices but in compartments or cubicles. Like a village, it was a close community—philosophers, mathematicians, biologists, household economists, historians, and so on, cheek by jowl—in which tensions were contained by necessity and a sense of common purpose. I found in our frequent discussions, and in others with my own department colleagues, a means of setting the university and its problems of the 1980s and 1990s in the context of a longer evolution from a private ecclesiastical institution into a state-funded (if only meagerly) secular one.

The problems I encountered were personal as well as institutional. The Department of History in the early 1980s was among the weakest in the university, judged if only on the basis of its low student-faculty ratio. It was also divided internally. If Frances and I can claim any part in the department's renaissance over the next decade or so—and I think we can claim quite a large part—it was not because we at first worked in unison. Tensions arose because another colleague, a friend of hers, was a temporary appointee who had to leave when Walter came into the department. Eventually the department could count collegiality, grounded in an acceptance of difference, among its strengths, but this was hard-won. More directly personal, I found reappointment, in an era when initial appointments were made on a term rather than a probationary basis, was only grudgingly given above the departmental level. The Dean, I discovered, had been disappointed that the department had chosen me over the internal candidate, and she took some time to get used to it. And having taught successfully in four other universities, I was taken aback by the difficulties I encountered in the classroom, though the chief complainant in my first year turned out to be the girlfriend of my rival for the job. I'm not sure Sister Patricia was aware of that. More than once in my early years at the Mount, at any rate, I found myself wondering if I had made the right decision in selling my bookstore.

In the department we gradually invigorated our program, though in the face of considerable obstacles. In my own area of Canadian history, our first attempt at reorganization was turned back at Curriculum Committee, after a tense open meeting—in those days, *all* course proposals were discussed at an open meeting of faculty—that resembled a bear-pit session more than anything else, or so it seemed to me, who played the role of bait. Our attempt to bring the curriculum into the post-World War II period almost foundered on the objections of departments who thought we were encroaching on their territory. One of my colleagues at the time, Nina Konczacki, who had a flair for dramatization, was fond of shaking her finger at me (and others) and warning in admonitory tones that one swam at the Mount in "shark-infested waters." The course changes were eventually made, along with many others. Aided by high enrolments in our two courses in the history of childhood, which were required (more or less) for students in Child Study, and by more new blood (Brook Taylor was appointed in 1986, on the retirement of Hugh Wallace), the department found new energy and new stability. We even introduced an honours program.

The practice of requiring students in professional studies programs, such as Child Study (as it was then called), to take courses in the humanities, sciences, and social sciences was one element of a building strategy promoted by the Fulton-Shelton duo—ably assisted by another of my eventual colleagues, Wayne Ingalls, a classicist now retired. Growth was anticipated in the expansion of professional studies (Public Relations was another example), whose programs were justified at the undergraduate level by extending their requirements beyond their specialized professional components, while the resulting enrolments in humanities, science, and social science courses helped to establish an enrolment base aiding in the development of individual programs in those disciplines. The strategy was by no means universally supported. Faculty in the traditional disciplines were often sceptical of the new programs and their place in a university (though programs like them had long been offered at the Mount and elsewhere), while faculty in the new ones were not always happy to give up spaces in their timetable to courses that seemed tangential to the needs of their professional practice. I often heard it said in those days that we were turning into a community college. In my own view, this was a strategy that made for productive interaction between professional studies and the liberal arts, and failure to nurture it in later years (and sometimes even to be aware of it) blunted the progress achieved in the late seventies, eighties, and nineties, and undermined collegiality.

One person who didn't fit neatly into any category was the director of the university art gallery, Mary Sparling, who invited me to join an advisory committee to the gallery in my first or second year. It was typical of her to reach out to new people in one way or another, and to draw them into gallery affairs. A few years later I participated in a panel on social history and photography organized by her friends Shelagh MacKenzie and Scott Robson; Shelagh was a force herself at the National Film Board and Scott at the Nova Scotia Museum.[146] Because of Mary, the gallery was a way not only into the Mount but into the cultural life of the city. Art for her was about audiences as well as art-makers, and the communities out of which art emerged. It was political, in the broadest sense, though not sectarian. She mounted shows that grew out of collaborative effort, and she assembled panels, symposiums, and conferences comprising people of different points of view. Perhaps the most famous of these was "Africville: A Spirit that Lives On," which brought together members of the African Nova Scotian community, politicians, journalists, and officials in a reassessment of the fate of Africville that seemed to me, as an outsider only a half-dozen years or so in Halifax, galvanizing in its impact. A similar thing happened around an exhibit about immigration through Pier 21 on the Halifax waterfront, which was the origin of a movement that culminated in the formation of the Canadian Museum of Immigration in 2011. Not least significant was her initiation of the Mount's annual community art show, where staff and students have an opportunity to show their work, or see the work of their friends and colleagues. Mary was a woman of great creativity and infectious enthusiasm, whose social conscience fit in with the community outlook of the Sisters of Charity.

The social commitment of the sisters was especially evident in the Mount's promotion of part-time study, aimed especially at mature women whose family responsibilities had prevented them from a more conventional—i.e. male—route to a university education. I found myself teaching evening classes just about every year, which always included older women who were more willing than their younger fellow students to ask questions and to disagree. They often stimulated their younger colleagues to take part in discussions. On a related front, Fulton picked up on Catherine Wallace's promotion of women's studies, which led to the establishment of the first department in Canada in 1986. She also supported Susan Clark, Dean of Human and Professional Development, and Wayne Ingalls in their plan to create an Institute for the Study of Women, which had come to fruition in 1981.[147] In my first few years at the Mount I taught my department's course in Canadian women's history, which I enjoyed until some students complained of being taught by a man!

I eventually found my feet and began to make myself a place in the university. I even put myself forward for Dean of my division at one point. Failure of my candidacy, coinciding with a job opening at Wilfrid Laurier, almost took me back to Ontario, but my family wouldn't hear of it. Shortly afterward, faculty unionized and I found myself in the spring of 1989 walking the Bedford Highway in front of the university with my colleagues (or most of them) in a strike provoked by the breakdown of negotiations for a first contract. This was an epoch-making event in the modern history of the Mount. Not only was a very good first contract eventually signed (negotiations on the faculty side having been led by Barnett Richling), which established much-improved procedures for appointment, reappointment, promotion, and tenure, among other things, but the experience of walking the picket line brought academic staff together in a new sense of collective purpose. This was our second attempt at unionization, the first having failed in 1983, and both attempts had inevitably produced divisions. By the second, however, some of the opponents of the first, such as Alleyne Murphy in the Department of Home Economics, the first lay faculty person ever appointed at the Mount, had grown impatient with administration practice, and the quiet determination of our association president, Margie O'Brien, commanded a wide following. In my last years at the Mount I served two terms as president of the Faculty Association.

The new sense of solidarity carried over into the nineties. A new university library was built—part of a new "communications centre"—and the collection was moved downhill from the its old Evaristus location. Even in the new space, however, many of the weaknesses in the collection that I had noticed ten years earlier remained. Prompted by faculty on the Senate Library Committee (and led more particularly by Brook Taylor), Senate passed a set of motions calling for carefully stepped increases in the library's acquisition budget, and we began building a collection appropriate to a modern undergraduate university, though it was still managed by a staff whose size was more appropriate to the old one. Meanwhile, Frances became for a time as much involved in Women's Studies as she was in History, particularly taking leadership in establishing and defining its program of study.

In the nineties I too found myself increasingly involved in policy issues, both as chair of my department and as a member of Senate and the Committee on Academic Policy and Planning, not to mention as a participant in two of the many planning "exercises" that recurrently occupied untold person-hours of administration and faculty time since the first was undertaken in the mid-1970s. I'm not entirely a Luddite when it comes to planning, but it has always seemed to me that much of what passes for planning goes on at a level that is stratospherically removed from what happens on the ground, and that it has its own intrinsic rationale and ends, which often contribute little to the solving of practical problems when they arise. Taking part in one of them ("Blueprint 98"), initiated by then-President Elizabeth Parr-Johnston, I sat on the committee on academic programs and our place in the provincial university system. The committee was chaired by Margie O'Brien and thankfully included such sensible people as Dale Godsoe, then chair of the Board of Governors, and other faculty members (Ann MacGillivary, David Furrow, and Chris Ferns). This was a process that actually worked quite well but my greatest pleasure was in working up a brief history of planning at the Mount in an attempt to set our efforts in some kind of perspective.

My perch in the History Department had grown more secure since the early eighties and was not a bad vantage point from which to observe what seemed to me a pretty constant round of challenges and changes. In response to a government task force, the education of teachers (then hugely in surplus) was consolidated, and the Mount managed to be designated the responsible Halifax training institution. Certain other departments went through their own mutations—Home Economics to Human Ecology to Applied Human Nutrition and Family Studies; Secretarial Arts to Information Management to Information Technology—while others changed their division, the social sciences joining with the humanities and sciences to form Arts and Science, leaving all Professional Studies programs in their own division, at least temporarily, until the later creation of the Faculty of Education. The provincial government introduced first a salary rollback then a salary freeze in the civil service and the universities, and cut its funding of post-secondary institutions, which in the Mount's case meant that our uniquely underfunded position, dating back to the financial arrangements that ended our private ecclesiastical status, was reinforced. One often hears that university faculty can't abide change. In almost thirty years at the Mount, I saw little else; much of it we initiated ourselves and all of it required our adaptation and implementation.

Through all of this change, however, the fundamental character of the university in its modern phase remained constant: dedicated primarily to the education of women, mainly undergraduate in its purpose with (in the words of the old mission statement) a liberal arts and science core and selected professional programs, and moved by a moral concern that had its origins in the stewardship of the Sisters of Charity but which had gradually secularized over time. Academic and non-academic staff were naturally the carriers of this tradition, which is not all that surprising. Some attributed the defense of the tradition by many academic staff in the planning debates to their inherent resistance to innovation, when in fact it represented their unwillingness to countenance a betrayal of values and practices that had been developed over more than a century, and that were the touchstone of their institutional attachment.

The literary theorist Northrop Frye, reflecting on his principalship of Victoria College in the University of Toronto in the late fifties and early sixties, said somewhere that the basic requirement of academic leadership was to serve as a "focus of articulation."[148] He meant by this that the beginning of one's job in any position of leadership in a university (though hardly the end) was to articulate—to promote and defend—the ideals, purposes, and functions of one's institution. This was uniquely required in universities, he thought, because their ideals and functions were socially necessary, yet so often intangible in their product, and because academic and non-academic staff worked best when they were secure in the knowledge that the significance of their work was recognized and defended. Students were also major beneficiaries of this leadership requirement. In my own philosophy of teaching I tried by my example, though very occasionally by explicit invitation, to draw students into a community of scholarship and intellectual endeavour. In my experience, those who take up the invitation are not only those at the top of their class, but right down through the grade ranks to the category of failure.

I am glad to say that I have heard many expressions of appreciation from my students for what they have learned in my classes, but the highest compliment I ever received was a remark from two very different students, an older man who had come back to university in retirement (free, or at least reduced, tuition for senior citizens in those days) and a young woman in her early twenties. They both said of my Historiography class—and these were two different classes a few years apart—that taking it was the first time they had really felt they were in university. I relate this, not to boast (though it was certainly very gratifying), but to urge upon university leaders that, rather than seeking to divine what they think students might want to hear, they instead articulate the high goals and high ideals to which they might aspire.

Left:
Megan and
Helen, 1990s

Left:
Marged and
Ken, Nova
Scotia, 1990s

Chapter Eight
Last Word

> None of us have identical memories of people. We all make up stories
> about those we love, or hate, just as we do about ourselves.
> —Ian Buruma, *Their Promised Land*[149]

One of my regrets about my personal life is that I never asked my mother about her life or my father's. This was partly because it simply didn't occur to me as a young person, and partly because I moved away from home when I grew older. I'm sure, nevertheless, that his death left a large hole in her existence. I was also sure of her love for me, but she was seldom demonstrative. The restrained temper of our household showed itself in various ways. I remember, for example, that when we moved back to the Highlands after my father died, my mother purchased a wringer washing machine to replace the automatic she had in the Trend House. She distrusted the quality of the job done by an automatic, and was instinctively suspicious of the gadgetry associated with it. Automatics were vaguely glamorous, at least as advertisers presented them, while wringers were functional and somehow more real as a result. Thrift played no small role in her preference. She had been brought up in a household that husbanded its resources, and the Depression arrived not long after her immigration to Canada. While our house did not suffer from the need to "tighten our belts," the memory of that need was ever-present, ready to be called upon to restrain anything that hinted of excess. There was dishwashing detergent available at the sink in the kitchen, but for a long time the normal means of preparing the water for doing the dishes was by vigorously shaking a device that had a small cage full of soap bits on the end of a wooden handle. The cage could be opened and closed by a simple spring and the soap bits were the remains of the bars we used in bathing or washing our hands. This was a method, we were told, that dated from the 1930s, and it achieved a mythic status in our family.

I remembered this when I read Joy Parr's study of washing machine consumption in Canada, part of her larger work on "domestic goods."[150] Struck by how it took substantially longer for automatic washers to dominate the market in Canada than it did in the U.S., Parr looked at differences in prices, disposable income, and domestic production, but concluded that the more extended dominance of wringers in Canada was only partly due to economic factors. It also had to do with the moral economy of the Canadian household. She was too late to interview my mother, but if she had, she would have received answers much like those she received from many women in the interviews she conducted as part of her research. Wringers were simpler machines, easier to repair and longer lasting, and they enabled a woman to keep track of her water consumption in order to avoid waste. They had value to offer in a consumer culture "habituated to scarcity and schooled to value conservation and thrift."[151] My mother's technological choice was a decision in favour of prudence over gratification (in Parr's terms), and it might stand for the moral economy in which I grew up. Needless to say, there was no question of acquiring a clothes dryer, which more slowly came into general use. Even when they became more common, Mom preferred to use the clothesline in the back yard. Dishwashers were not even up for consideration.

It is risky to attribute too much influence to upbringing in shaping an adult life. The twists and turns of my own life have been the result of changing circumstances and associations. At the same time, there has also been a continuity of temper rooted in my family and the years of my growing up. Woody used to make a habit of interjecting the phrase, "moderation in action and attitude," always in an ironic tone of voice, at appropriate moments in conversation during car pool trips to and from the University of Alberta in the early sixties. The rest of us chuckled appreciatively. It was a variation on the ancient maxim, "Moderation in all things," slyly (and acutely) modified in more modern times by Oscar Wilde to read, "Everything in moderation, including moderation." It represented an outlook that stayed with me, if sometimes inconsistently, throughout my life, as I was reminded recently when another friend and longtime colleague at Mount Saint Vincent, Brook Taylor, recommended a book by the Romanian-American political scientist, Aurelian Craiutu, *Faces of Moderation: The Art of Balance in an Age of Extremes*. Craiutu takes on the job of defending moderation, not merely as a position adopted midway between extremes, though that can be its effect, but as an approach in itself to political debate and decision-making.[152] It does not mean that one is weak-kneed, mealy-mouthed or opportunistic; moderates, on the contrary, can be strong-minded, principled, and committed. Nor does it necessarily mean that one's politics are centrist; it is possible to be a moderate on the left or a moderate on the right. All of this struck me as eminently sensible when I read the book, capturing, as well, the temper of my own views, conservative and radical, over the years.

Craiutu acknowledges that moderation is difficult to define in the abstract and shows what he means through studies of five leading European thinkers of the twentieth century: the Russian-British historian and philosopher Isaiah Berlin, the French sociologist Raymond Aron, the Italian philosopher Norberto Bobbio, the English philosopher Michael Oakeshott, and the Polish historian and dissident Adam Michnik. All of them were active public intellectuals, none could be accused of being weak-kneed, and most of their thinking, despite their many differences, was marked by a disposition toward scepticism and an aversion to dogmatism. They also displayed qualities of character essential to moderation, including prudence and civility. Aron was widely known in the sixties, but also widely dismissed in the left-wing circles I inhabited as "just" a liberal, while Oakeshott's conservatism pushed him to the margins as well. Somehow, I avoided this blinkered outlook in the case of Berlin, the only one of these men whose work I knew at all well, partly because of his interest in the philosophy of history, which interested me as well, and partly because I admired the breadth and depth of his knowledge and interests, which included Russian intellectual history.[153]

Moderates, in Craiutu's argument, accept the imperfections of human beings and the need for politics, defined as an activity that seeks compromise and conciliation among groups who have their own interests and uphold their own truths. This is a view that has close affinities with that of Bernard Crick, the British political scientist and a moderate of the left himself. I read his small (but eventually much expanded) book, *In Defence of Politics*, many years ago and was struck by its realism, wisdom, and calm assessment of the alternatives to politics, such as ideology and nationalism. Crick approached politics, as Craiutu approaches moderation, as a thing in itself. "Politics," he wrote, "arises from accepting the fact of the simultaneous existence of different groups, hence different interests and different traditions, within a territorial unit under a common rule."[154] Reaching some sort of agreement or accommodation among these groups called for the same personal and intellectual qualities that Craiutu associates with moderation, summed up sharply by Adam Michnik as "a mixture of sinfulness, saintliness, and monkey business."[155]

Anyone who has studied the history of Canadian politics can't help but smile in recognition. I taught my share of courses in the subject during the course of my career and was often dismayed by the prevalence among my students of an image of Canada and its politics as unbearably dull, compared with the drama of so many other countries, notably the U.S. Recurring efforts were mounted, by writers such as Pierre Berton, to deny its dullness and prove its excitement and attraction. I often used to say to my students in response that Canadian history was indeed dull, but that's what made it interesting. I didn't mean by this to encourage complacency or to diminish the importance of conflict, oppression, and injustice in Canada's past. I only meant to suggest that the country's relatively stable order, and the practice of politics at the centre of its public affairs, did not imply an absence of courage and inventiveness among its politicians. Isaiah Berlin wrote at one point that, "The middle ground is a notoriously exposed, dangerous, and ungrateful position," and Craiutu uses the quotation as the epigraph of his chapter on Berlin.[156] This has been recurringly evident in Canadian politics, along with the monkey business.

Berlin was also fond of quoting the philosopher Immanuel Kant on human nature: "Out of timber so crooked as that from which man is made nothing entirely straight can be built."[157] The idea of the crooked timber of humanity provided a foundation of his moderation. Perfect solutions were beyond human ingenuity, as likely to lead to suffering—hardly uncommon in the course of the twentieth century—as to failure. This offers little comfort to anyone seeking simple remedies, or to those who think they are in the absolute right and their opponents in the absolute wrong. It is a salutary thought, however, and consistent with the outlook I acquired as a young man, even if I did not always adhere to its wisdom.

Acknowledgments

I am indebted to many people for reading and commenting on the manuscript of this book: to my wife Marged, my daughters Megan and Helen, and my brother Bob; to my friends Terry Copp, Brian Dippie, Elwood Johnson, Dale Miquelon, the late Blair Neatby, Ruth and Mark Phillips, Barnett Richling, David Stafford, and Peter Ward. I thank them all very much. I would also like to thank Barnett for his assistance with the photographs,

Notes

Chapter One

1. Julian Barnes, *The Sense of an Ending* (Toronto: Random House Canada, 2011), 40.
2. Carl Becker, "Everyman his own Historian," *American Historical Review*, 37, 2 (January 1932), 221–36; J. H. Hexter, "The Historian and His Day," *Political Science Quarterly*, 69, 2 (June 1954), 219–33, reprinted in *Reappraisals in History: New Views on History and Society in Early Modern Europe* (New York: Harper Torchbooks, 1963 [1961]), 1–13.
3. "Hilda Neatby and the Ends of Education," *Queen's Quarterly*, 97 (Spring 1990): 36–51.
4. Ibid., 48; Hilda Neatby, *So Little for the Mind* (Toronto: Clarke, Irwin and Co. Ltd., 1953), 326.
5. Neatby, *So Little for the Mind*, 232 (emphasis in original).
6. "Hilda Neatby's 1950s and My 1950s," *Journal of Canadian Studies*, 40, 1 (Winter 2006): 210–31. The earlier essay was "Hilda Neatby and the Ends of Education," *Queen's Quarterly*, 97 (Spring 1990): 36–51.
7. "Alberta Advantage: A Memoir," *Alberta History*, 61, 1 (Winter 2013), 2–9; "Bookselling in a Small Town, " *The Nashwaak Review*, 36/37, 1 (Summer/Fall 2016), 302–9.
8. Barnes, *The Sense of an Ending*, 4.

Chapter Two

9. Obituary (Maxwell C. Dewar), Royal Architectural Institute of Canada *Journal* [*RAIC Journal*], 32 (May 1955), 186.
10. *Edmonton Journal* [*EJ*], 2 Apr. 1955.
11. Michael Kurtz, "Trend House Chronicles," <http://mkurtz.com/trendhouse/history/index.html>.
12. Trevor Boddy, *Modern Architecture in Alberta* (Regina and Edmonton: Canadian Plains Research Centre and Alberta Culture and Recreation, 1987), 83.
13. *EJ*, 3 April 1954.
14. City of Edmonton Archives [CEA], RG 11/21/30, Memorandum from G.S. Doherty, City Clerk, to City Commissioners, 24 Nov. 1953 (Re: Choice of Architect for proposed new city hall); Edmonton City Clerk's Office, Contract of Agreement between The City of Edmonton and Maxwell C. Dewar, John Stevenson and K.C. Stanley, 30 March 1954 (see Sec. 12).
15. *EJ*, 27 Apr. 1954.
16. City of Edmonton, *Your New City Hall* (n.p., [31 May 1957]), 2.

17. Personal correspondence from Harold Sprague, 18 Apr. 1988; Dudley B. Menzies, n.d.; Hugh W. Seton, 28 Oct. 1988; K.C. Stanley, 15 Dec. 1988.
18. EPCOR Power Development Corporation and EPCOR Generation Inc., "Rossdale Power Plant Unit 11 (RD 11), Application No. 990289," May 2001, 38 <http://www.auc.ab.ca/applications/decisions/Decisions/2001/2001-33.pdf>.
19. Canada's Historic Places, "Rossdale Power Plant" <http://www.historicplaces.ca/en/rep-reg/place-lieu.aspx?id=5896&pid=9067&h=Edmonton>; Alberta Register of Historic Places, Alberta Heritage Survey Program, Rossdale Power Plant, <https://hermis.alberta.ca/ARHP/Details.aspx?DeptID=2&ObjectID=HS%2075869>.
20. Rossdale ReGeneration <http://rossdaleregeneration.ca/>.
21. *Vue Weekly*, 11–17 Oct. 2018.
22. See, for example, Marianne Fedori, Ken Tingley, and David Murray, "The Practice of Postwar Architecture in Edmonton, Alberta: An Overview of the Modern Movement, 1936–1960" <http://issuu.com/davidmurrayarchitect/docs/inventory_master_report_1>.
23. Canada's Historic Places, "Churchill Wire Centre" <http://www.historicplaces.ca/en/rep-reg/place-lieu.aspx?id=3010&pid=6449&h=Edmonton>; Edmonton's Architectural Heritage, "Churchill Wire Centre" <http://www.edmontonsarchitecturalheritage.ca/structures/churchill-wire-centre/>.
24. Murray, "The Practice of Postwar Architecture," 48.
25. J. G. MacGregor, *Edmonton: A History* (Edmonton: Hurtig Publishers, 1967), 283.
26. "President's Address, Annual Meeting Alberta Association Architects January 23, 1948," RAIC *Journal*, 25 (March 1948), 94.
27. Erna Dominey, "Wallbridge and Imrie: The Architectural Practice of Two Edmonton Women, 1950–1979," *Society for the Study of Architecture in Canada Bulletin* 17, 1 (March 1992), 15 <http://sextondigital.library.dal.ca/jssac/PDFs/Bulletin/Vol.17/vol17_no1_OCR_150dpi_PDFA1b.pdf>.
28. Dominey, "Wallbridge and Imrie," 17.
29. David Murray and Marianne Fedori, "Overview of the Practice of Architecture in Edmonton 1930–1969" and "Buildings by Area, Northeast Edmonton, Victoria Composite High School," in *Capital Modern: A Guide to Edmonton Architecture and Urban Design 1940–1969* <http://capitalmodernedmonton.com/>.
30. Art Evans, "Edmonton's Proposed City Hall," Calgary *Albertan*, 1 May 1954.
31. Walter Johns, *A History of the University of Alberta 1908–1969* (Edmonton: University of Alberta Press, 1981), 246–8.
32. Edmonton Exhibition 1958 <http://www.youtube.com/watch?v=15-lxHGziok>.
33. CEA, Minutes of Civic Centre Committee Meeting, 11 Dec. 1953, Memorandum from M.C. Dewar, Dewar Stevenson, and Stanley attached.
34. The Edmonton City Hall is one of the buildings used to illustrate the International Style in Shannon Ricketts et al., *A Guide to Canadian Architectural Styles*, 2nd ed. (Peterborough, ON.: Broadview Bress, 2004 [1992]), 196.
35. CEA, M.C. Dewar to His Worship Mayor William Hawrelak, 30 April 1954 and reply, 6 May 1954; see also the Memorandum from M.C. Dewar cited above.
36. *EJ*, 3, 6, 14, 27 Apr. 1954.
37. Kenneth C. Dewar, "Just a tempest in a teapot," *EJ*, 23 Nov. 1988.
38. Trevor Boddy, "Postscript," in *Capital Modern: A Guide to Edmonton Architecture and Urban Design 1940–1969* <http://capitalmodernedmonton.com/postscript/>.

Chapter Three

39. Alberta Teachers' Association, Religious and Moral Education Council <http://www.teachers.ab.ca/For%20Members/Professional%20Development/Specialist%20Councils/Council%20Directory/Pages/Religious%20and%20Moral%20Education%20Council.aspx>
40. Tom Hawthorn, "Musician Wes Dakus was Edmonton's answer to Elvis," *Globe and Mail*, 25 Oct. 2013.
41. *Edmonton Journal*. 25 Apr. 1960.
42. Lawrence Herzog, "Edmonton's Original Burger Kings," <http://www.rewedmonton.ca/news/2004/01/15/edmontons-original-burger-kings>
43. Colin K. Hatcher, *YMCA of Edmonton: The First One Hundred Years*, 52 <http://www.northernalberta.ymca.ca/Portals/0/pdfs/history_book_web_version.pdf>.
44. Margaret Atwood, *Survival: A Thematic Guide to Canadian Literature* (Toronto: House of Anansi, 1972), 73–5.
45. Daniel Francis, *The Imaginary Indian: The Image of the Indian in Canadian Culture* (Vancouver: Arsenal Pulp Press, 1992), 146.
46. Ibid., 149, quoted.
47. Sharon Wall, *The Nurture of Nature: Childhood, Antimodernism, and Ontario Summer Camps, 1920–55* (Vancouver: UBC Press, 2009), 217–18.
48. *Edmonton Journal* [*EJ*], clipping, n.d. [1964].
49. Hedley S. Dimock and Charles Hendry, *Camping and Character: A Camp Experiment in Character Education* (New York: Association Press, 1929).
50. Ibid., 41.
51. Wall, *Nurture of Nature*, 251, 255, 257.
52. Myrna Kostash, with Duane Burton, *Reading the River: A Traveller's Companion to the North Saskatchewan River* (Regina: Coteau Books, 2005).
53. Wall, *Nurture of Nature*, 218.
54. Paul First Nation <http://www.paulfirstnation.com>.
55. Ken Dewar, "The Road to Happiness: Canadian History in Public Schools," *This Magazine is About Schools*, 6 (Fall 1972), 102–27.
56. Francis, *The Imaginary Indian*, 168.

Chapter Four

57. Wallace D. Farnham, "The Study of American History in Canada Universities," Canadian Historical Association *Annual Report*, 37, 1 (1958), 67.
58. Gerhard J. Ens, *Canadian History at the University of Alberta: In Honour of the Generation Now Retiring from University Service* (Edmonton: n.p., 2012), 17–18.
59. Barbara Fraser, "The Political Career of Sir Hector Louis Langevin," *Canadian Historical Review*, 47, 2 (June 1961): 93–132.
60. Ens, *Canadian History at the University of Alberta*, 31.
61. Donald Wright, *The Professionalization of History in English Canada* (Toronto: University of Toronto Press, 2005), 100.
62. George Grant, *Lament for a Nation: The Defeat of Canadian Nationalism* (Toronto: McClelland and Stewart, 1965).
63. John G. Diefenbaker, *One Canada: Memoirs of the Right Honourable John G. Diefenbaker*, 2 vols. (Toronto: Macmillan, 1975 and 1976).
64. Paul Rutherford, *When Television was Young: Primetime Canada 1952–1967* (Toronto: University of Toronto Press, 1990), 516 n.2; Morris Wolfe, *Jolts: The TV*

Wasteland and the Canadian Oasis (Toronto: James Lorimer & Co., 1985), 80–4.

Chapter Five

65. Heidi MacDonald, "Transforming Catholic Women's Education in the Sixties: Sister Catherine Wallace's Feminist Leadership at Mount Saint Vincent University," *Encounters in Theory and History of Education*, 18 (2017), 53–77.
66. Lara Campbell and Dominique Clément, "Introduction: Time, Age, Myth: Towards a History of the Sixties," in Lara Campbell, et al., *Debating Dissent: Canada and the Sixties* (Toronto: University of Toronto Press, 2012), 6–7.
67. Doug Owram, *Born at the Right Time: A History of the Baby Boom Generation* (Toronto: University of Toronto Press, 1996), 189.
68. John Haslett, "Acts of Attention: What Susan Sontag Never Changed Her Mind About," *The New Yorker*, 11 Dec. 2017, 75–80.
69. Donald Wright, *Donald Creighton: A Life in History* (Toronto: University of Toronto Press, 2015), 9.
70. Ralph Heintzman, "Political Space and Economic Space: Quebec and the Empire of the St. Lawrence," *Journal of Canadian Studies*, 29, 2 (1994), 19.
71. Duncan McDowall, "David Farr," Toronto *Globe and Mail*, 23 Nov. 2016.
72. A.R.M. Lower, *Colony to Nation: A History of Canada* (Toronto: Longmans Green, 1946), xiii.
73. Richard M. Saunders, "Presidential Address," *Historical Papers/Communications historiques*, 2, 1, (1967), 1.
74. *Toronto Star*, 4 June 1966.
75. George P. Landow, *Elegant Jeremiahs: The Sage from Carlyle to Mailer* (Ithaca, NY: Cornell University Press, 1986).
76. Mark Phillips and Ken Dewar, "The Professionalization of History," *This Magazine is About Schools*, 5, 1 (Winter 1971): 34–58. A version of my part was also published in a review of Creighton's *Canada's First Century*, "Nationalism, Professionalism and Canadian History," *Canadian Dimension*, 7, 5 & 6 (Dec. 1970): 71–4.
77. Gad Horowitz, "Conservatism, Liberalism, and Socialism in Canada: An Interpretation," *Canadian Journal of Political Science*, 32, 2 (May 1966), 143–71.
78. Louis Hartz, *The Founding of New Societies: Studies in the History of the United States, Latin America, South Africa, Canada, and Australia*, with contributions from Kenneth C. McRae, et al. (New York: Harcourt, Brace, 1964).
79. "George Grant was 'wrong, wrong, wrong,'" *Globe and Mail*, 17 Apr. 2009.
80. Catherine Dunphy, "He helped bring CanLit to the world," *Toronto Star*, 28 Mar 2005 [Gordon Roper obituary].
81. Sandra Djwa, *Professing English: A Life of Roy Daniells* (Toronto: UTP, 2002), 310–13; see also Nick Mount, *Arrival: The Story of CanLit* (Toronto: Anansi, 2017), 74.
82. "Technology and the Pastoral Ideal in Frederick Philip Grove," *Journal of Canadian Studies*, 8, 1 (Feb. 1973), 19–28.
83. Elizabeth Greene, "A Walk Among the Dead," in *Understories* (Toronto: Inanna Publications, 2014), 88–93.
84. *Toronto Daily Star*, 8 April 1968.
85. "Pierre Elliott Trudeau and the Liberal Party: Continuity and Change," *Canadian Dimension*, 5, 5 (June–July 1968), 7–9.

86. Peter Russell (ed.), *Nationalism in Canada* (Toronto: McGraw-Hill, 1966).
87. Ian Lumsden (ed.), *Close the 49th Parallel etc: The Americanization of Canada* (Toronto: University of Toronto Press, 1970).
88. MacDonald, "Transforming Catholic Women's Education in the Sixties," 55.
89. Andrew Todd and Franco La Cecla, "Ivan Illich" [obituary], *The Guardian*, 9 Dec. 2002.
90. "Inventory of the Latin American Working Group (LAWG) Fonds," Clara Thomas Archives, York University <http://archivesfa.library.yorku.ca/fonds/ON00370-f0000463.htm>.
91. Andre Gunder Frank, *Capitalism and Underdevelopment in Latin America: Historical Studies of Chile and Brazil* (New York: Monthly Review Press, 1967 [1966]).
92. For example, Paul A. Baran, *The Political Economy of Growth* (1968 [1962]), Paul A. Baran and Paul M. Sweezy, *Monopoly Capital: An Essay on the American Economic and Social Order* (1968 [1966]), and Harry Magdoff, *The Age of Imperialism: The Economics of U.S. Foreign Policy* (1969), all published by Monthy Review Press.
93. John Porter, *The Vertical Mosaic: An Analysis of Social Class and Power in Canada* (Toronto: University of Toronto Press, 1965); on Porter, see Rick Helms-Hayes, "Engaged, Practical Intellectualism: John Porter and 'New Liberal' Public Sociology," *Canadian Journal of Sociology*, 34, 3 (2009), 831–68).
94. Catherine Gidney, "War and the Concept of Generation: The International Teach-ins at the University of Toronto, 1965–1968," in Paul Stortz and E. Lisa Panayotidis (eds.), *Cultures, Communities, and Conflict: Histories of Canadian Universities and War* (Toronto: University of Toronto Press, 2012), 275.
95. Myrna Kostash, *Long Way from Home: The Story of the Sixties Generation in Canada* (Toronto: James Lorimer and Co., 1980), 46.
96. Donald Evans, "The Diplomacy of a Teach-in," in Charles Hanly (ed.), *Revolution and Response: Selections from the Toronto International Teach-in* (Toronto: McClelland and Stewart, 1966), Appendix, 133–40.
97. Gidney, "War and the Concept of Generation," 278–9.
98. Quoted in A.B. McKillop, *A Disciplined Intelligence: Critical Inquiry and Canadian Thought in the Victorian Era* (Montreal and Kingston: McGill-Queen's University Press, 1979), 232.
99. Charles Hanly, "Introduction," in *Revolution and Response*, viii.
100. Staughton Lynd, "Ideology and the New Left," 114 and Fenner Brockway, "Moral and Political Aspects of Dissent," 131 in Hanly (ed.), *Revolution and Response*.
101. George Grant, "Protest and Technology," in Hanly (ed.), *Revolution and Response*, 123–8.
102. Cheddi Jagan, "A Case Against American Involvement," in Hanly (ed.), *Revolution and Response*, 25

Chapter Six

103. *The Realist*, 74 (May 1967); "Paul Krassner.com" http://www.paulkrassner.com/.
104. Noam Chomsky, "A Special Supplement: The Responsibility of Intellectuals," *New York Review of Books*, 23 Feb. 1967; Robert R. Tomes, *Apocalypse Then: American Intellectuals and the Vietnam War, 1954–1975* (New York: New York University Press, 1998), 152.

105. Peter Russell (Ed.), *Nationalism in Canada* (Toronto: McGraw-Hill, 1966), xix; Kenneth C. Dewar, *Frank Underhill and the Politics of Ideas* (Montreal and Kingston: McGill-Queen's University Press, 2015).
106. Stephen Azzi, "The Nationalist Moment in English Canada," in Lara Campbell, et al., *Debating Dissent: Canada and the Sixties* (Toronto: University of Toronto Press, 2012), 213.
107. Allan Smith, "Metaphor and Nationality in North America," *Canadian Historical Review*, 51, 3 (Sept. 1970), 275.
108. "The Waffle Manifesto: For an Independent Socialist Canada," No. 6 and 7 <http://www.connexions.org/CxLibrary/Docs/CX5372-WaffleManifesto.htm>.
109. James Laxer, *Red Diaper Baby: A Boyhood in the Age of McCarthyism* (Vancouver: Douglas and McIntyre, 2004).
110. Roberta Lexier, "'The Backdrop Against Which Everything Happened': English-Canadian Student Movements and Off-Campus Movements for Change," *History of Intellectual Culture*, 7, 1 (2007) <https://www.ucalgary.ca/hic/issues/vol7/3>.
111. Philip Resnick, "The New Left in Ontario," *The New Left in Canada*, ed. Dimitrios J. Roussopoulos (Montreal: Our Generation Press, Black Rose Books, 1970), 96, 107–8.
112. Graduate Alumni, Slavic Languages and Literature, Yale University, George M. Young <http://slavic.yale.edu/graduate-alumni>.
113. Solomon Volkov, *St. Petersburg: A Cultural History*, trans. Antonina W. Bouis (New York: The Free Press, 1995), xii.
114. Quoted in Catriona Kelly, *Remembering St. Petersburg* (Triton Press, 2014), 44 <http://oxford.academia.edu/CatrionaKelly>.
115. The entire poem can be found in John Owen Theobald, "'The Muses Were Not Silent': Leningrad and the Poetry of the Siege," Laurier Centre for Military Strategic and Disarmament Studies, Blogs, 10 Jan. 2013 <http://canadianmilitaryhistory.ca/the-muses-were-not-silent-leningrad-and-the-poetry-of-the-siege-by-john-owen-theobald/>.
116. Masha Gessen, *The Future is History: How Totalitarianism Reclaimed Russia* (New York: Riverhead Books, 2017), 166; Anthony Beevor, "The Unmentionable Season of Death," *New York Review of Books*, 18 Jan. 2018, 43–4; see Gregory Carleton, *Russia: The Story of War* (Cambridge, Mass.: Harvard UP, 2017), Ch. 3 "The Burden of Victory," 80–113. An even darker picture of present-day Russia, internally and externally, is offered by Timothy Snyder, *The Road to Unfreedom: Russia, Europe, America* (New York: Tim Duggan Books, 2018).
117. Dmitri Shvidkovsky, *St. Petersburg: Architecture of the Tsars*, photographs by Alexander Orloff, trans. from the French by John Goodman (New York: Abbeville Press Publishers, 1996), 190–3.
118. The State Hermitage Museum <http://www.saint-petersburg.com/virtual-tour/hermitage/>.
119. My memory of this meeting was somewhat confused until Jud clarified it for me in an email exchange not too long ago.
120. Anna Ivanova, "Shopping in Beriozka: Consumer Society in the Soviet Union" *Zeithistorische Forschungen/Studies in Contemporary History*, 10, 2 (2013), 243–63. *Beriozka* is Russian for birch tree.
121. H.V. Nelles, *The Politics of Development: Forest, Mines and Hydro-Electric Power in Ontario, 1849–1941* (Toronto: Macmillan, 1974).

122. "State Ownership in Canada: The Origins Of Ontario Hydro" (Ph.D. thesis, University of Toronto, 1975); "Toryism and Public Ownership: A Comment," *Canadian Historical Review*, 64, 3 (Sept. 1983), 404-19.
123. Howard Adelman and Dennis Lee (eds.), *The University Game* (Toronto: Anansi, 1968). The Bissell quotation is from a blurb on the back cover.
124. Patricia Jasen, "'In Pursuit of Human Values (or Laugh When You Say That)': The Student Critique of the Arts Curriculum in the 1960s," in Paul Axelrod and John Reid (eds.), *Youth, University, and Canadian Society: Essays in the Social History of Higher Education* (Montreal and Kingston: McGill-Queen's University Press, 1989), 247-9.
125. Report of the Committee on the Reappraisal of the Graduate Programme in History, 19 July 1968.
126. Kenneth McNaught, *Conscience and History: A Memoir* (Toronto: University of Toronto Press, 1999), 23.
127. Report of the Graduate History Society on the Re-appraisal of the Graduate Programme in History, 3 Oct. 1968; University of Toronto, Department of History, Report of the "Committee of Eight" on the Report of the Graduate Appraisal Committee [n.d., November 1968]
128. *The Primary Source*, 2, 2 (10 Dec. 1969).
129. Robin Mathews and James Steele (eds.), *The Struggle for Canadian Universities* (Toronto: New Press, 1969).
130. Department of History "Teach-In" [n.d.]; *The Primary Source*, 1, 1 (1 Dec. 1969).
131. E.g. *The Primary Source*, 2, 2 (10 Dec. 1969) and 3, 3 [n.d.]; "Faceless Committee must not judge us 29 professors say," *The Varsity* [clipping, n.d.]
132. Jill Ker Conway, *True North: A Memoir* (New York: Alfred A. Knopf, 1994), 157-8.
133. My thanks to Brian Dippie for correcting my memory of this progression.

Chapter Seven

134. Robert Bothwell, et al., *Canada since 1945: Power, Politics, and Provincialism*, rev. ed. (Toronto: University of Toronto Press, 1989 [1981]), 367-74.
135. Denis Smith, *Bleeding Hearts ... Bleeding Country: Canada and the Quebec Crisis* (Edmonton: M.G. Hurtig Publishers, 1971).
136. Pierre Vallieres, *White Niggers of America*, trans. Joan Pinkham (Toronto: McClelland and Stewart, 1969).
137. *The Martlet*, University of Victoria, 28 Jan. 1971.
138. John Eklund, "David Stimpson, book traveler," *Paper Over Board*, 17 Oct. 2010 <http://paperoverboard.blogspot.ca/2010/10/david-stimpson-book-traveler.html>.
139. David Wesley, "Elora: A quaint little success story," Hamilton *Spectator*, 21 June 1980.
140. Nick Mount, *Arrival: The Story of CanLit* (Toronto: Anansi, 2017), 82, quoted.
141. Ibid., 25-6.
142. Peter R. Sinclair and Kenneth Westhues, *Village in Crisis* (Toronto: Holt, Rinehart and Winston, 1974).
143. "ABA Membership Profile 1977," reprinted from *American Bookseller*, Jan.-Feb. 1978.
144. *Charles Clarke, Pen and Ink Warrior* (Montreal and Kingston: McGill-Queen's University Press, 2002).

145. Theresa Corcoran, SC, *Mount Saint Vincent University: A Vision Unfolding 1873–1988* (Latham, MD: University Press of America, 1999), 59.
146. "Historians and historical photographs: 'Why look at this stuff?,'" in *Social History and Photography: The Atlantic Region, 1870–1920*, Proceedings of a symposium held at the Art Gallery, Mount Saint Vincent University, 22–23 March 1985 (Halifax: Mount Saint Vincent University Art Gallery, 1990): 37–43.
147. Corcoran, *Mount Saint Vincent University*, 277.
148. John Ayre, *Northrop Frye: A Biography* (Toronto: Random House, 1989).

Chapter Eight

149. Ian Buruma, *Their Promised Land: My Grandparents in Love and War* (New York: Penguin Press, 2016), 18.
150. Joy Parr, *Domestic Goods: The Material, the Moral, and the Economic in the Postwar Years* (Toronto: University of Toronto Press, 1999), Ch. 10, "What Makes Washday Less Blue?" 218–42.
151. Ibid., 241.
152. Aurelian Craiutu, *Faces of Moderation: The Art of Balance in an Age of Extremes* (Philadelphia: University of Pennsylvania Press, 2017).
153. For example, *Four Essays on Liberty* (Oxford: Oxford University Press, 1969); *Karl Marx: His Life and Environment* (Oxford: Oxford University Press, 1963); *Russian Thinkers*, ed. Henry Hardy and Aileen Kelly, intro. Aileen Kelly (Harmondsworth, Middlesex: Penguin, 1979). See Michael Ignatieff, *Isaiah Berlin: A Life* (Toronto: Viking, 1998).
154. Bernard Crick, *In Defence of Politics*, 2nd ed. (Chicago: University of Chicago Press, 1972 [1962]), 18.
155. Craiutu, *Faces of Moderation*, 160, quoted.
156. Ibid., 60.
157. Ibid., 84, quoted; Isaiah Berlin, *The Crooked Timber of Humanity: Chapters in the History of Ideas*, ed. Henry Hardy (New York: Knopf, 1991).

Index

aboriginal rights, 93
Adelman, Howard, 125
Alberta Association of Architects, 7, 19, 22
Alexander II, Tsar, 114
Amankwah, Kofi, 49
Ancestry.com, 15
anti-Americanism, 69, 105-9
Anderson, Harold, 72
Appeldoorn, Beth, 138, 144
Arbat, 119
Aron, Raymond, 163
Askinas, Barry, 135
Atwood, Margaret, 42
Avonmore United Church, 26
Axelrod, Paul, 4
Azzi, Stephen, 106-7
Bailey, Rich, 45
Banff, 9, 34
Banff Springs Hotel, 9
Barnes, Julian, 1, 5
Beatles, 105
Beattie, Norman, 121
Beck, Adam
Becker, Carl, 1
Berger, Carl
Berlin, Isaiah, 163, 164-5
Bliss, Michael
Boddy, Trevor, 28
Bociurkiw, Bohdan, 65
Bookselling, 137-140
Borden, Robert, 105
Brockway, Fenner, 99, 101
Brother Bonaventure, 56
Brown, George, 34
Brown, Robert Craig, 62-3, 73, 97, 105, 132
Burger King Drive-In, 38-9
Burgess, Cecil, 7, 19, 22
Burt, A. L., 65
Byrne, Cyril, 124
Camp Keewaydhin, 39-50
Canadian Broadcasting Corporation, 71-2
Canadian Dimension, 95, 98

Canadian literature, 89
Canadian nationalism, 69-70
Cardinal, Harold, 93
Careless, Anthony, 121
Careless, J. M. S., 82
Carleton University, 82, 147
Carnegie, Dale, 38
Cawston, John, 19
Charles, Dean
Chernyshevsky, Nicolai, 88
Chomsky, Noam, 104
Churchill Wire Centre, 21
Clarke, Charles, 146-7
Clarke, Garry, 79-80, 91
Claus, Helen and Clare, 139
Club Stardust, 35-6
Cluff, David, 81
Cohen, Leonard, 90, 105
Conway, Jill, 129
Cook, Ramsay, 85-6, 95
Copp, Terry and Linda, 136, 137, 147
Cowan, Charles, 73-4, 131, 136
Craiutu, Aurelian, 163
Creighton, Donald G., 4, 82, 83, 86-7
Crick, Bernard, 164
Cromdale Community Rink, 8
Cromdale School, 31
Cummings, Al, 141
Czechoslovakia, Soviet invasion of, 119-20
Dakus, Wes, 36
Dalhousie University, 131
Dartmouth College, 109
Davies, Robertson, 80
Davis, Natalie, 128, 129
Dean, Stanley, 37
Delta Upsilon, 52-3
Dewar, Helen, 5, 79, 145
Dewar, Mary B., 7, 161-2
Dewar, Maxine, 9, 10, 14-5
Dewar, Maxwell C., 7ff.
Dewar, Megan, 79, 145
Dewar, Robert (Bob), 8, 14

Dewar, Violet, 9
Dewar Stevenson and Stanley, 7, 8, 17, 25, 26
Dewey, John, 3, 46
Dickinson, Catherine, 139
Diefenbaker, John, 69–70, 106
Dimock, Hedly S., 45–6
Dippie, Brian, 67, 72, 73, 132, 136
Drain, Susan, 152
Dyck, Harvey, 127–8
Dylan, Bob, 104
Dyster, Barrie, 94
Early, Frances, 148, 157
Eastglen High School, 32, 37–8
Eastwood, Terry, 73
Eccles, W.J., 34, 59, 61
Edmonton City Hall, 17–8, 26–9
Edmonton Gardens, 32
Edmonton Exhibition Grandstand, 26
Edmonton Junior Mystic Circle, 51
Edinburgh, 13
Eisenstein, Sergei, 119
Elora, 137–140, 144
Elorabooks, 141, 142–7
Elora Heritage Festival, 143
Ens, Gerhard, 58
Evans, Art, 25
Farnham, Wallace, 56, 59
Farr, David M. L., 82
Fielding, Marna, 16
Forbes, Ernie, 132
Foster, John, 97–8, 127
Frank, Andre Gunder, 98
Francis, Daniel, 42, 50–1
Fraser, Barbara, 59–63
Friesen, Gerald, 81, 90, 124, 131
Frye, Northrop, 158–9
Fuhr, Cap, 40
Fulford, Robert, 85–6
Fulton, Margaret, 150–1
Glasgow, 13
Gonick, Cy, 95
Gooch, Stan, 73
Gordon, Walter, 106
Grant, George, 3, 70, 86–7, 99, 101
Greene, Elizabeth, 92
Greenock, 11
Griffiths, Naomi, 148
Grove, Frederick Philip, 90
Guthrie, Gwen, 37
Hades, Mickey, 53
Hallman, Diane, 4
Hamilton, Alvin, 70
Hanly, Charles, 99–101
Harney, Dale, 52
Hart House, 93–4
Hartz, Louis, 87
Hawrelak, William, 17, 27
Hayden, Michael, 2
Heeney, Brian, 68
Helmstadter, Richard, 88–9
Hendry, Charles E., 45–6
Hermitage Museum, 115
Heron, Craig, 127
Hexter, J. H., 2, 72
historian, role of, 84–5
Hood, Hugh, 100
Horowitz, Gad, 87, 122
Houdini, Harry, 51–2
Houston, James, 12
Houston, Matthew, 13
Houston, Robert, 12
Hrychuk, Bill, 34–5
Hurtig, Mel, 106
Illich, Ivan, 96–7
Imrie, Mary, 23–4
Ingalls, Wayne, 154
International Brotherhood of Magicians, 4, 51
International Style, 27
Jasen, Patricia, 125
Jarrett, Merrick and Mary, 143
Johnson, Elwood, 20–1, 32, 37, 162
Johnson, Lyndon, 69, 103
Jones, W. J., 58
Kealey, Greg, 127, 128
Kennedy, Jacqueline, 103
Kennedy, John F., 67–8, 103
Kilpatrick, Willam H., 46
King, Martin Luther, 68, 77
Knudstrup, Nancy, 139, 143
Konczacki, Nina, 153
Kostash, Myrna, 49, 99
Krassner, Paul, 103
Krupa, Gene, 33
Kubesh, Donald, 92–3, 131, 136
Lang, Bob, 51
Laxer, James, 107
Lee, Dennis, 125
Lencek, Lena, 116, 117
Leningrad, 110–8
liberalism, 94
Litt, Paul, 4
Long, Morden H., 58, 65
Lower, A. R. M., 83
Lumsden, Ian, 94–7, 131
Lynd, Staughton, 99, 101
MacCallum, Dr. James M., 44
Macdonald, John A., 105
MacDonald and Magoon, 19

MacFarlane, Karen, 63
MacKinnon, Ken, 124
MacLean, Greg, 68
Macpherson, C. B., 94
Mandel, Eli, 65, 90
Marxism, 102, 107–8
Massey, Vincent, 2–3
Massey College, 80
Mathews, Robin, 65, 124, 128
Maxwell Dewar Building, 19–21
McClelland and Stewart, 69
McDowall, Duncan, 82
McKeen, Grant, 45, 48–9
McKenna, Frank, 73
McKillop, Brian, 100
McLaughlin, Ken, 131
McLean, Bunny, 32
McNaught, Kenneth, 126, 128
McNeal, Robert H., 56–7, 88, 109
Melnikov, George, 65, 109
Menzies, Dudley, 18, 23
Michnik, Adam, 164
Miliband, Ralph, 99
Millar, Hugh Paton, 16
Millar, James, 11–12
Millar, Janet, 10
Millar, Matthew, 11, 16
Miller, Bob, 144–5
Miller, Jim, 4
Minifie, James M., 71, 79
Miquelon, Dale, 2
Miss Edmonteen Ball Association, 36–7
Mitchell, Joni, 94, 105
moderation, 162–5
Morton, W. L., 86
Moscow, 118–9
Mount, Nick, 140
Mount Saint Vincent University, 29, 77–8, 148; history department, 129–30, 149; unionization, 156
Mullins, Sister Patricia, 149, 153
Murphy, Alleyne, 156
Neatby, Hilda, 2–3, 24, 78, 100
Neatby, H. Blair, 4, 148
Nelles, Viv, 122
Newman, Peter C., 106
O'Brien, Margie, 156, 157
Overton, Pat, 32, 36–7
October Crisis, 133
Ontario Hydro, 121–2
Owram, Doug, 78
Ozawa, Seiji, 105
Parr, Joy, 162
Partridge, Bruce, 134–5

Payer, Pierre, 77–8, 152
Peacock, Thomas Love, 89
Pearson, Lester, 70, 106
Pedersen, Eileen, 138
Peers, Sue, 34
Phillips, Mark, 77, 86, 127, 131
Phillips, Ruth, 127, 131
Pitsula, James, 4
Porter, John, 98–9
Prentice, Allison, 4
Purves-Smith, Michael, 143
Realist, The, 103
Rebel Without a Cause, 14
Resnick, Philip, 108
Richling, Barnett, 152, 156
Roper, Gordon, 89
Rosengrant, Judson, 116, 117
Rotstein, Abraham, 100, 106
Royal Architectural Institute of Canada, 7
Rubin, Donald, 90–2, 131–2
Sarick, Judy, 141
Saunders, Richard, 85
Seba Beach, 10
Seton, Ernest Thompson, 42–3
Seton, Hugh, 18, 27
Shelton, Walter, 151
Shugarman, David, 71
Singleton, George, 45
Sir Daniel Wilson residence, 80
Sisters of Charity of St. Vincent de Paul, 149
Smith, Allan, 107
Sparling, Mary, 154–5
Sprague, Harold, 40, 50
Stacey, Col. Charles, 60
Stafford, David, 132
Stanley, Kelvin, 7, 18
state ownership, 121–3
Statten, Taylor, 43, 46
Stelter, Gilbert, 56
Stimpson, David, 137, 145
student politics, 123–30
Symons, T. H. B., 90
Taylor, Brook, 154, 156, 163
Tbilisi, 119
Thomas, Lewis G., 56, 58
Thomas, Lewis H., 58, 63
Thomas, Marged, 93
Thompson, E.P., 88–9
Thompson, Fred, 139
Thomsom, Tom, 44
Three Centuries Festival, 143–4
tory collectivism, 87
Treaty of Washington, 72–3
Trend House program, 8

Trudeau, Pierre Elliott, 43, 94–5
Underhill, Frank, 84, 106
Union of Soviet Socialist Republics, 109–121
United Church, 35
United Nations Association Seminar, 34
University College, 80
University League for Social Reform, 96
University of Alberta, 2, 55; history club, 65–7; history department, 55–65; library, 64
University of Toronto, 2, 74, 81–90
University of Victoria, 131–6
Vallieres, Pierre, 133
Vanderhaeghe, Guy, 5
Van Kirk, Sylvia, 66
Vasey, Lyn, 142
Vienna, 120
Vietnam War, 87, 99, 104
Victoria Composite High School, 24–5
Volkswagen 1500, 79, 91

Voyageur Camp, 47–50
Waffle Movement, 107, 135
War Measures Act, 133–4
Wall, Sharon, 44-5, 47, 50
Wallace, Catherine, 97, 150–1
Wallbridge, Jean, 19, 23–4
Ward, Peter, 24, 32, 37–8
Watkins, Melville H., 100, 106, 107, 135
Weber, Max, 35
Westfall, William, 29
Wien, Thomas, 4
Wildgoose, Nancy, 93, 131, 136
Wolfe, Tom, 103
women's studies, 155–6
Wright, Donald, 4, 66
Wynn, Gordon, 18
Yevtushenko, Yevgeny, 113, 116–7
Young, George, 110
Y's Men's Club, 8, 39

www.ingramcontent.com/pod-product-compliance
Lightning Source LLC
Chambersburg PA
CBHW072157070526
44585CB00015B/1189